Keep Singing

Keep Singing

Two Mothers, Two Sons, and Their Fight Against Jesse Helms

By Patsy Clarke and Eloise Vaughn
with Nicole Brodeur

Foreword by Allan Gurganus

alyson books
los angeles | new york

MANUFACTURED IN THE UNITED STATES OF AMERICA.

THIS TRADE PAPERBACK ORIGINAL IS PUBLISHED BY ALYSON PUBLICATIONS,
P.O. BOX 4371, LOS ANGELES, CA 90078-4371.
DISTRIBUTION IN THE UNITED KINGDOM BY
TURNAROUND PUBLISHER SERVICES LTD.,
UNIT 3, OLYMPIA TRADING ESTATE, COBURG ROAD, WOOD GREEN,
LONDON N22 6TZ ENGLAND.

FIRST EDITION: MAY 2001

01 02 03 04 05 a 10 9 8 7 6 5 4 3 2 1

ISBN 1-55583-572-4

LIBRARY OF CONGRESS CATALOGING-IN-PUBLICATION DATA
CLARKE, PATSY.
    KEEP SINGING : TWO MOTHERS, TWO SONS, AND THEIR FIGHT AGAINST
JESSE HELMS / BY PATSY CLARKE AND ELOISE VAUGHN, WITH NICOLE
BRODEUR.—1ST ED.
    ISBN 1-55583-572-4
    1. MOTHERS AGAINST JESSE IN CONGRESS (POLITICAL ACTION COMMITTEE)—
HISTORY. 2. CLARKE, PATSY—POLITICAL ACTIVITY. 3. VAUGHN, ELOISE—POLIT-
ICAL ACTIVITY. 4. PARENTS OF AIDS PATIENTS—UNITED STATES—CASE STUD-
IES. 5. HELMS, JESSE—VIEWS ON AIDS (DISEASE). 6. HELMS, JESSE—VIEWS
ON GAY MEN. 7. HOMOPHOBIA—UNITED STATES—CASE STUDIES. 8. POLITI-
CAL CAMPAIGNS—NORTH CAROLINA—CASE STUDIES. I. VAUGHN, ELOISE.
II. BRODEUR, NICOLE. III. TITLE.

HQ76.45.U5 C58 2001
306.874'3—DC21

CREDITS
•LYRICS TO "LET IT BE THE SONG" USED BY PERMISSION OF CHRISTIAN
 BENSCHOP DAVENPORT.
•COVER PHOTOGRAPH OF PATSY CLARKE AND ELOISE VAUGHN BY ROGER
 WINSTEAD.
•COVER DESIGN BY MATT SAMS.

To the memory of our sons,
Mark Russell Clarke and Mark Foster Vaughn

To my son Sawyer Brooks Donahue,
for the boy he is and the man he will become

CONTENTS

"The second rule of magic: Things which were once in contact with each other continue to act on each other after the physical contact has been broken."
—Sir James George Frazier, *The Golden Bough*

"Where, after all, do human rights begin? In small places, close to home."
—Eleanor Roosevelt

ACKNOWLEDGMENTS

Much of this journey has been arduous and much has been joyous.

The following wonderful people have walked with us all the way, and we thank them all:

Our families: Candy Clarke, Judy Clarke, Speedy Rice, Bruce and Diana Clarke, Marilynn Clarke Williams, Mace Graham, Stuart and Shay Vaughn, John and Cheri Vaughn, and Rose Vaughn Williams and her husband, Jon.

Our many friends and supporters, among whom are Allan Gurganus, Lee Smith, Betty DeGeneres, John Shelby Spong, Charles Frazier, Elizabeth Birch, Bob Page and Dale Frederickson, Rob Bilbro and Stuart Brock, Kevin Layton, Holly Schadler, Susan Parker, Memsey Price, Tim Kirkman, Charles Ashby, Art Sperry and his elves, Harriet Grand, Sally Wade, Betsy Hunt, Jeff Lawson, Eliza Taylor and Kathy Tritschler, Flora Isasi, Mitchell Foushee, Michael Armentrout, Cara Benedetto, Cullen Gurganus, Jimmy Creech, Donna Red Wing, Wade and Ann Smith, and Mark Donahue.

Tests and Blessings: A Duet for Altos
A FOREWORD BY ALLAN GURGANUS

Along with physical comfort, all sane people want some chance at moral grandeur, but such challenges can be hard to come by in a house quite this upholstered! Financially, we're not exactly insecure, we're blessed with our own health and with several lively advanced placement children—kids whose orthodontia we guess we can afford, however bucked their teeth! We only make ourselves drinks at 5 sharp (though we've been primed since 3). Then, sitting back, ice clinking, we half long for the Test.

Some real—if brief and vivifying—ethical dilemma. A personal conundrum would try our mettle now that the Underground Railroad's been derailed, now that all of history's major wars seem won. We watch, on rental video, safe at home, Anne Frank's family hiding in their freezing attic storeroom. And we wonder if we're the kind of secular saints who would risk our own lives to save the lives of folks not like us. Sure, we know that smooth lawns and Harvard early admissions aren't anybody's natural birthright. And yet the more grateful we guiltily feel, the sharper grows this secret hope for some single challenge, one as large as our own luck. Our luck till now...

Would we, say, hide others from the Nazis? Maybe

Hitler's sole helpful contribution was providing the ultimate "what if?" nightmares that still blast open our happy-hour daydreams.

Such imagined wartime Tests rarely last as long as even a feature film. The folks we're asked to save are always strangers. We either open the door, or we really don't. And since it's all fantasy, since we each find so many clever daily ways to remain the heroes and heroines of our lives, we usually "do the right thing." At least while we view ourselves in '40s black-and-white on-screen...

But what if we ranked among the vast German majority? I mean the group that sensibly bolted its doors, that drew the draperies, then hid in the foyer keeping very quiet till strangers' poundings either drew the soldiers' jackboots or till such troublemakers swerved their Test toward a neighbor's darkened house?

The authors of this work are two otherwise happy, healthy, not-unlucky women. Till it found them, they'd never thought to listen for such midnight slammings, not from the brass knockers of their neocolonial doors. Attractive, well-educated, articulate, upbeat whenever possible, they were each born to a class that owns more often that it rents. In their poise and goodwill, they remind me of my mother's closest friends during those more secure 1950s. Such women were often far brighter—far more emotional and imaginative—than their highly respected husbands. Such women held genuine opinions (if ones often silenced half-voluntarily). They lived in true relation to both literature (a book group of long standing) and religion (Episcopalian, Presbyterian). And yet they held back: "Isn't it better not to bore or corner other people with one's own views?"

The authors each possess the kinds of organizational skills that might run multinational corporations. Instead, you'd have usually found them waiting for their kids' piano lessons to end, sitting in each other's cars, quietly communing, laughing often—with a sense of humor that sometimes seems God's greatest gift to any of his creatures, the Tested and the un-Tested-as-yet.

Outsiders might view such lives as cozy to the point of stultifying. Security can grow same-ish as a "good" block's side-by-side manicured lawns. These women lived in Raleigh, N.C., the secure state capital known for its side-street oaks and aged dogwoods, but they moved in slightly separate circles. And yet they would soon meet—these underrated people so successfully disguised to themselves and others as mere, if absolute, "ladies." They remained strangers till a pounding on two separate doors eventually united them. By the time they joined forces, they had both been harrowed, chiseled, and dignified by an identical Test.

It would slither right into an "older neighborhood." It would shamingly slam against no other door along this handsome block. This pair would be subjected, in a time of peace, to a trial that must rank with those the Nazis continue to provide our gloomy drama-queen imaginations:

"Whom would I defend? Might I not keep silent to save myself and my other beloved kin? How strident dare I be so I might keep my value as a helper? How 'political' is too political? At what point must I abandon my lifetime edict to remain 'understated' and 'attractive' in order to do raw and unappealing but genuine good?"

This book seems to tell us this: Those people in the world most fully alive—the ones most rueful if most wise—are often the folks who've already outfaced and endured their great Test. Those who somehow—energy spent but self-esteem still woozily intact—managed to acquit themselves during the dread and unsought visitation.

Let this cup pass from me, even Christ begged. But in the end, he drank it, he saw mortality through. Likewise, blessed are the Christians called upon to act like, actually, Christ. Not the spun-sugar blue-eyed Jesus in robes fluffed white as a fresh-whipped vanilla milkshake. No, I mean the dusty Middle Eastern wanderer, a man "not comely and acquainted with grief." I mean the healer-savior in filthy sandals who, new to town, always sought out not the mayor and the owners of the camel dealerships, but hurried straight to sinners, to the fallen, to those most unpicturesquely sick.

How different such behavior from a pretty city's usual church rules: the white country-club congregation membership, a casserole brigade with new outfits on Christmas and Easter and other fashion-calendar upgradings timed to coincide with major events in the life of our suffering Christ.

I don't want to give away the story of the Test. You must read it for yourself. Think of this book as a letter sent you by friends. The authors' fond, bright, kindly, childlike first names are still Patsy and Eloise. Always good to hear from them. Their letter's tone is so offhanded, funny, essentialized, now casual, now urgent. We overhear family jokes, nicknames, running stunts, the topsy-turvy everydayness of suburban lives with bright kids at their centers. This is a book by people who have not written other books but simply had to set down this one. It's a work borne along by their doubled emotional currents. It is a work that sneaks up on you like the surprise ending of some amazing bulletin from your own home.

You must hear the story in the voices of these brave,

enlarged, and luminous women—warriors themselves. Their tale is a fable and a promise of development. Because life is so fraught with nighttime shocks, we're never too secure, too settled, too old to learn. The story involves adored sons. Both were named Mark. Each of them loved the theater. Each was fair and lank and handsome, always the most warmly charismatic guest at any party, at every family dinner after church.

This is a story of two Tested mothers' growth. They began with a trusting good-girl faith in conventional religion, in politics as usual. They believed in the essential decency of the important men always in charge of both our church and state.

One of the heroines is a "yellow-dog Democrat" (meaning, of course, she'd vote for any ole yellow yard dog before choosing even a human-appearing—if secretly gilled—Republican). Our other leading player was a somewhat unexamined—I mean, un-Tested—Republican. That could be changed! She and her husband had been personal friends of the senior senator from North Carolina, a Mr. Jesse Helms. He is a man renowned for his personal decency and for the contrast that makes when set alongside his long history of opposing black people's civil rights, equal pay for women, money for the Third World, reproductive rights, government funding for the arts, our nation's dues owed the U.N.—a man averse to spending a single penny of federal money to cure AIDS or help its victims. To my mind, the list of the movements Mr. Helms has tried to thwart reads like the inventory of those 20th-century advances that might, when our poor history is written, help offset the Nazi exterminations of Jews and gay people, help balance a matching public cowardice that allowed this to roll on for years, unchecked.

The senator has always understood how few steps separate the grassy greens-fee consolations of "us" from the dark tangled zone of sinners, of those so repellently sick that only a Christ could love. Only Christ. Or a mother.

The appealing young sons of the authors had spent perhaps a few years extra "finding themselves." Then, just as the boys seemed to gain a bit of peace and direction, they each made an announcement. Within separate wallpapered homes, using a single-blasted pair of sentences their moms would later call "the double whammy," the beloved sons told how they were (a) gay and (b) already sick with AIDS.

Certain Test choices at once arose. This was not some midnight stranger banging at a door. It was not even one's well-liked Jewish green grocer or clock repairman begging for a moment's shelter in your basement's half-bath. No, here stood one's own flesh and blood, a person born with visiting privileges, a kid improved by orthodontia and endless skin procedures and lessons in dressage and the piano. Someone you loved had just turned from a blond boy of easily assumed privilege to membership in not one but two of the most despised fringe groups in the world. What to do? With him? *For* him?

One of the classic images of 19th-century melodrama shows a strict farmer-father sending his unwed daughter and her newborn out into a snowstorm. She weeps, bundled in her shawl too thin. He stares well beyond her, a Christian man of principle, pointing to the nearest rutted country lane. He refuses to accept the pleading gaze of his recent favorite.

And, listen: The patriarch does not banish his child and grandchild to certain death *despite* his religious and moral convictions. No, he does it *because* of those. Some

Protestant stringency has long since convinced him: Punishment outranks acceptance. Sufficient shame can always override love. Jesus' lessons have been utterly inverted (and all in the name of His church).

This is where Senator Helms comes in. You might be surprised to learn how many contemporary parents, like Helms, blamed the victims. When their children arrived home sick with AIDS, they blocked the very doorways and pointed elsewhere, anywhere. Then, having sent their own off to die in a charity ward, these elders retreated indoors, turned up the thermostat, said a prayer, and felt a little better about themselves. They'd just passed God's latest Test! They had not been sentimental but strong.

We are now 20 odd years into the pandemic; amazing new drugs prolong vigorous lives. A culture so amnesiac as ours can hardly recall the medieval thinking and superstitious primitivism that attended this disease's emergence.

One way to remember? Go read the speeches Sen. Jesse Helms made on the floor of the U.S. Senate. The Good Book tells us about our own flawed natures: "Let he who is without sin cast the first stone." Christ himself, purportedly guiltless, chose to assume blame in order to be counted fully human. But Senator Helms...as a boy in Angier, N.C., as the spindly son of a stern local sheriff, young Jesse must have been sick the Sunday this essential text was taught.

Surely no pitcher in the National League has scored more strikeouts with more stones. What a great rock pile of ammo Helms has assembled in the nearly four decades that my fellow North Carolinians have been sending him again and again to the pitcher's mound of the World Series to rock-hurl in our name.

It must be a mixed blessing to consider yourself so completely guiltless. Especially of that major crime called being human. Helms resisted any funding for curing a new disease experts first tried to name "gay cancer." Its earliest victims were, conveniently, Haitians and frisky, young, urban gay men. Two populations completely—indeed, conveniently—expendable.

By such logic, if the person pounding on your door is a Jew and you a Christian, you need not open said door. You need not even wake to the sounds of screamed panic. If they're in such trouble with the police, there must be a reason. And since we are still safe indoors, and since the deadbolt's holding solid, all we need do now is remain motionless. They will either go away or the police must hear such a racket and come clear them off our doorstep like so much refuse tidily removed. End of ethical debate? Are they "us"? No. Merely "THEM." Case closed.

If this disease had first attacked blond Baptist Raleigh dentists whose incomes exceeded 100K and whose golf scores were usually below 100, no firebrand would've been more evangelical in his pulpit-pounding fervor on the Senate floor. Helms would have proven as fierce in his demands of funding for these men's health as…well, as he has been for the rosy-pink health of the tobacco industry.

Fact is, the senator never guessed that sons of his own club and church friends might catch such a disease. One of this book's authors had earlier received handwritten sympathy notes and kindly little cards from Senator Helms. And so, still trusting the man's essential humanity and Christian ethos, when she heard him using the U.S. Senate as a forum to define gay people as corrupt predators who deserved their painful deaths, she sat down and wrote him. She urged him to cease such vilification. She politely asked him to please support funding for AIDS research. She reminded him that she was a social acquaintance of long standing. When she identified her son as a sufferer, Helms's personal note in response left no doubt about *his* us vs. *her* them: "I am sorry he chose to play Russian roulette with his sexuality."

Part of the heartbreak of this earnest, essential book is the faith its authors first placed in those white men placed so completely in charge—of the people's government and of Christ's own church. To these women's credit, soon as they sized up the depth of bigotry arrayed against their sudden cause, they—in a crash course of on-the-job training—grew independent fairly fast. They soon found among official Republicans and Democrats alike requests and then commands to keep quiet about a topic inconvenient, ugly, awkward. But by now, for the authors, "should be seen but not heard" would no longer do. However embarrassed by their roles, however many parties they silenced by simply mentioning a disease and its relation to their own children, they were fighting to save the lives and bodies of their loved ones. Certain standard thank-you-note niceties soon came to seem a little shallow. But along with rejection, they found whole new communities of love. And they—bless them—were soon inventing their own way to tread a path between the ladylike and the rude, between their own good breeding and a terrible need to hurry, hurry...

They went on to found MAJIC, Mothers Against Jesse in Congress. They recruited for its ranks other mothers still shell-shocked from the worst grief of all, a living parent's longing for a perished child.

Few people have the courage to open that door at the first knock, fewer still to pull in the despised one then bolt that portal. But love for their sons was too great to endure the separation of "us" and "them." A group of resourceful, tony moms soon took on many of the responsibilities that a decorous timorous church and our poll-consulting legislators shirked during this disease's early days.

Soon, opening that door seemed easy compared to the bedside vigils, the washings, the admission of decline, the conquering of one's hoping against hope for good news personal, medical, governmental.

This you hold in your hand, then, is a tale less dispiriting than inspirational. To *inspire* means literally "to breathe into." These mothers did that more than once. First they gave their sons life. Then they reenlisted. They provided their kids a good safe place to be, somewhere warm from which young men might slide back to childhood then infancy and beyond their own beginnings. All attended by their own first sponsor...

The book you hold now is a gift. From two lionesses in good linen suits. And from two boys named Mark. These are the guys who knew all verses of every show tune, the lives of every party. This record can now offer you, in the spoken language of these charming, decent, intelligent, energized women, a chronicle of pain endured, of pain somewhat transcended but never ever ever forgotten. Their collective tale, told in alternating chapters the way courteous talkers take turns, has the quality of a mouth-to-ear exchange and finally a mouth-to-mouth transfer of life. This is the tale of how two mothers, belatedly finding their own children in mortal trouble, were changed by their instant struggle to help.

When the door Tested is your front door, you don't have time to stand there and debate the moral nuances of man's inhumanity to man and whether to risk your ass. You throw the door open and pull the fugitive through it into your safety, your *former* safety. Or else, you don't. Good people have done both.

But here are two who risked every staid assumption, two who helped. Because they felt they had to. They take no credit. They offer the story because it so deserves saving. In saving it, they seek to save the best of their charming sons.

Some list-loving church folks will tell you that the truly godly people are the ones who live so correctly, so much by the letter of the law, that they are never questioned, never thwarted, never grieved nor tried by messy and unseemly experience. Their children all have children, preferably blond ones who soon shoot golf scores in the low 80s and get into Princeton and live to be 110, with a portfolio big enough to take care of lawn-care expenses, clear to the end. Such optimists are dead wrong.

The luckiest people in the world are those who see the trouble, who instantly know that trouble and who come to love its features, who soon learn trouble's every talent, its own complete potential. Such people live forever after opened to the world, not hidden forever within gated communities behind the great moats and steeples and civic edifices protecting all that's safely "us."

Blessed are those who—asked to defend, forced to become pushy and too visible and overly shrill on behalf of someone wasting toward looking 99 at the age of 27—somehow find they *can*.

Loving someone makes you deeper, wider, more nimble, and—when your beloved is attacked—fiercer, if you're lucky. Nothing is more politicizing than really loving another person. And when they get into terrible trouble thanks to an unjust law, there's no telling how Christlike you, his defender, might have to grow. Nothing is more radical and righteous and clever than a mother defending, Portia-like, her child wrongly accused and otherwise abandoned. And no one needs to read this book more than a certain senior senator. Shame on him for dealing all these decades in code words for the despised minorities. Pity his soul for having trafficked so cynically all these years in such daily punishment and shame.

You are about to hear the story of two people who, subjected to the most paralyzing of news, still somehow scaled a path of action—and while wearing fairly high heels! Two women were Tested but not found wanting. These mothers proved worthy of Christ's true lessons and of their own children's faith. There comes to all of us—if maybe only at the moment of our mortal exit—a Test.

May we each prove as worthy of ours as these clear spirits have been to their unasked-for agonizing mission. This book is not just an account of a Test; it is yet another repayment and annex of that unending Test itself.

May their amazement—gone to outrage, become conviction and then pure angelic action—embolden even the best-bred of us to grow still bolder in our kindness. May we be less passive-gentle-milky in our love. May we swoop—more transitive—to the defense of whatever latest group is so irrationally loathed. May we work harder still to unseat those officials who see hating and withholding as their surest way to reelection.

Here are two souls who found a way to speak, then shout, and finally—in honor of their show-loving boys—to, against all odds, create a kind of moral vocal music. You are about to hear a duet for altos. Untrained voices, the kind sweetest and truest with an essential melody. Their music is part "Onward, Christian Soldiers," part "I Wanna Be Around to Pick Up the Pieces," part "A Boy's Best Friend Is His Mother." It is a cry of pain—both tin-pan alley and pure hymn.

And may it become a "standard" for those forced to act, answer, and grow. Because they could not stop loving.

World without end. Amen.

INTRODUCTION

Keep Singing explores the journey of Eloise Vaughn and Patsy Clarke, two grandmothers who spent 1996 trying to unseat one of the most powerful politicians in America: Sen. Jesse Helms of North Carolina.

Their story begins more than 30 years ago, when their sons, both named Mark, were born and raised in upstanding Southern families. While they grew up in politically opposite households, the sons shared the same secret and, eventually, the same fate: Both were gay, and both contracted and succumbed to AIDS with their mothers at their sides.

These two mothers represent thousands of parents of their generation who raised their sons well and at a certain point stopped asking questions. When boys became ill with that terrible disease their parents had only read about in *Newsweek,* it changed everything. And those parents, like Clarke and Vaughn, rose to the occasion; they stood to battle AIDS while their friends were settling into easy chairs to watch *Wheel of Fortune,* the kids long gone, their work done. They fought the disease and accepted that AIDS was in their lives, not for political or moral reasons—but because they loved their sons.

The deaths of Mark Clarke and Mark Vaughn brought two very different women together in mourning and into a relationship that would evolve into a deep friendship, sudden activism, a new purpose, and, ultimately, inner peace.

It is ironic that the story is set in North Carolina, a comfortable Southern land where deep-brown soil grows fine tobacco, pigs grow fat, and folks still clean and press white shirts for Sunday services. Here, Jesse Helms has built his legend as the fiery senator who never leaves you guessing about his politics. He is marble-mouthed and homely, conservative and arch, but folks believe Helms stands for all they work for: home and family and the way things should be. And when it comes to AIDS and homosexuals, well, that just isn't right. And no one states that more clearly to them and to the nation than Jesse Helms.

He is a man who has mastered the art of making politics personal, of looking out into a crowd and getting people to nod their heads, because he's one of them, isn't he? He has a house in Raleigh, right off Glenwood Avenue. Shops at the old Piggly Wiggly when he's in town, eats the vegetable plate at Joe's Mom's Place. He is one of the most powerful men in the country, but he is still a good ol' boy.

Jesse Helms went a little too far for Patsy Clarke. He got a little too personal. The same man who called Clarke in the middle of the night to offer condolences when her husband was killed in a plane crash said that men like her son deserved to die.

Those words changed everything. They shed a harsh glare into the warm glow of Clarke's retirement years and forced her to question everything she had come to believe. They made her better, stronger, and more understanding. And they brought her one of the finest friendships she has ever known.

This book chronicles how two mothers with vastly different political viewpoints dealt with their sons' homosexuality in very similar ways, for both were hit with the double whammy: "I am gay, and I am HIV-positive."

Initially, the revelation meant instant damage control: Not only were they concerned with saving their sons from a wrenching, painful death, but Clarke and Vaughn also had to put aside everything they had expected from life, everything they had known: the neat, clubby alliances they had built through decades of church and professional involvement; the legacies of propriety left by their late husbands, who both had traveled in political inner circles.

All at once these tradition-bound women were faced with managing the specter of homosexuality and the dark, sinister grip of AIDS: a drawn-out, debilitating illness that crawled through their two beautiful sons while they could do nothing but comfort and soothe. Motherhood would make one final, glorious rally before Clarke and Vaughn would watch their sons go.

They were brought together by a mutual friend who knew of their losses—and then by a phone call.

"My name is Eloise Vaughn, and I understand you've lost a son to AIDS," she would say that night. "So have I."

They met, they mourned, they told their stories, and then they organized a support group of mothers whose sons had died of AIDS. It seemed to help, but then there was nothing to do but cry for dead men. They didn't seem to be moving ahead.

Then Vaughn came across a newspaper article in which Helms, the man who had put North Carolina on the political map—for better or for worse—was quoted implying that AIDS victims deserved what they got.

Vaughn showed the clipping to Clarke, her Republican friend, whose late husband, Harry, had been a friend of

Helms's and had worked on his campaigns. It was Helms who had called Clarke in the night after her husband died in a plane crash. It was Helms who'd had the flag flown over the capitol in honor of her husband and then sent it to her.

In June 1995 Clarke wrote to Helms, thanking him for his friendship. And then she told him of her son, Mark, how he had been gay and died of AIDS. She asked that Helms be more compassionate toward people with AIDS—for her, for Harry, and for their son.

"My reason for writing to you…is to ask you not to pass judgment on other human beings as 'deserving what they get.' No one deserves that. AIDS is not a disgrace, it is a tragedy. Nor is homosexuality a disgrace; we so-called normal people make it a tragedy because of our own lack of understanding."

Two weeks later, Helms wrote back:

"I know that Mark's death was devastating to you. As for homosexuality, the Bible judges it, I do not. As for Mark, I wish he had not played Russian roulette with his sexual activity. I have sympathy for him and for you. But there is no escaping the reality of what happened."

With those words, the two grandmothers found purpose, a clear path through the haze of losing a child and into the political arena and the AIDS battlefield. They decided to fight Jesse Helms's reelection.

As founders of Mothers Against Jesse in Congress (later known as MAJIC), Vaughn and Clarke found that their differing political ideologies suddenly no longer mattered.

Clarke, to her own surprise, became what she had always called a "wild-eyed liberal." She drifted from her faith and conservative beliefs to face down a political giant, a man her family had long identified with and considered a political advocate and friend.

The women sought support at gay bars. They held rallies that felt more like church socials than rabble-rousing sessions. They attended the Democratic National Convention, shared a stage with Sen. Ted Kennedy, and listened to endless stories from mothers just like themselves—and from their sons.

There is no storybook ending, unfortunately. Helms was reelected and is now the powerful chairman of the Senate Foreign Relations Committee. But Vaughn and Clarke won nonetheless: They helped others to gain strength in acknowledging and taking pride in their gay children, every one of them loved and wonderful.

"It all happened on a dark and stormy night," Clarke likes to say, "when the winds of change blew us out of the kitchen with all of the good smells and into a societal world with the rankest of odors: homophobia."

That night grew into a day of clear reasoning and understanding, and of raising some simple truths:

Being gay just is. It is not a tragedy or a disgrace.

Parents have the freedom to love their children no matter what.

And finally, the truth can be liberating, for it frees you. It frees you to live.

—*Nicole Brodeur*

PROLOGUE

As this book was being written, Eloise found herself at a dinner party of friends she had known for many years. They knew she had cofounded Mothers Against Jesse in Congress and that a book about that campaign was in the works.

Over dessert and coffee, the hostess turned to her and said, "Tell us about your book, Eloise." All the faces turned to her, open and waiting.

She began with our meeting and resulting friendship. She talked about our sons and the "double whammy" each of us had received: At the same time our sons told us they were gay, they also told us they were HIV-positive.

Eloise spoke of how two mothers with differing political views dealt with their sons' homosexuality. She explained the view held by Sen. Jesse Helms that "people who died of AIDS deserved what they got," and how that resulted in my "Dear Jesse" letters and, eventually, the formation of MAJIC.

She described our trip to Chicago, where we spoke at one of the meetings held in connection with the 1996 Democratic National Convention. She told them how a small group of mothers in Raleigh, N.C., had made such a bold effort on behalf of their late sons that they received support across the nation. And she acknowledged that we had lost the election but found a greater goal.

This book, she said, is an extension of that goal. It is

our continuing campaign on behalf of families—because that is how we see this issue.

When Eloise finished speaking, she was aware of her heart pounding in her chest. No one had interrupted her No one had asked a question. No one had made a comment. There was just stillness. She looked around at the faces of her lifelong friends and waited.

Finally, a voice said, "You know this is going to be very controversial, don't you?"

Several days later, Eloise related this story to me and said that we had better expect this kind of reaction.

We were sitting in our favorite restaurant having the Monday special of spaghetti and meat sauce. I've never been very adept at twirling my pasta, and as I considered what Eloise had just said, I put the big spoon down, inhaled what was on my fork, and tasted renewed resolve. "And what is controversial," I asked, "about loving your children and being proud and accepting of them?"

If *Keep Singing* is controversial, so be it. But what we have written about is of universal concern. There is no family, no classroom, no gathering—social or business—that is unaffected by the issue of tolerance.

Behind the statistics of those who have died of AIDS or who are suffering from it, of those who have been stigmatized because of their homosexuality are individual people with real personalities, real fears, real loves, and real miseries.

There is no controversy about this. And there is no controversy that cannot be helped by compassion and an effort at understanding. This is the story of our effort. Take our hands and walk along with us.

—*Patsy Clarke*

About the Title

My grandmother had a song she sang to me, and it went like this:

Rock-a-bye and don't you cry,
Rock-a-bye, little Patsy.
I'll buy you a pretty gold horse
To ride all around your pasture.

As each child in our family was born, this lullaby belonged to him or her and had that child's name in its midst. I would sing, rock, and comfort until sleep came, the fever waned, or our time together had worked its magic.

As my son, Mark, was suffering the grand mal seizure that presaged his death at age 31, I stood at the foot of his hospital bed, rubbing his bare feet and instinctively singing that baby song. The medical team surrounded him, trying to restrain him and save him.

In those stark, white moments, I suddenly became aware of the incongruity of that baby song, coupled with the sight of my adult son dying, and I stopped singing. A nurse looked up at me and shouted, "Keep singing!"

Without knowing why, I started to sing again, and I sang and I sang and I sang until I could sing no more, and Mark was finally calmed.

So that's why the title of this book became *Keep Singing*. Eloise and I both feel that we were privileged to sing to our children when they were babies

We now feel that we are privileged to keep singing in their memories.

—*Patsy Clarke*

Chapter One

MARK CLARKE, SUPERMAN

Mark Clarke stood out in a crowd, both figuratively and literally. At 6 foot 7, he was always the tallest person in the room unless, of course, he found himself in the Celtics' locker room. But given Mark's interests, that was highly unlikely.

Because his death has so obsessed the rest of my days, I sometimes forget that he had a life, which is not fair. He had a wonderful bunch of years. Granted, there were not enough of them, but those he had were top-notch.

Isn't it funny how we humans say that our dear departed were happy, fun to be around, above average in every way, and many other glowing descriptions that were often denied them in life? Well, here goes another human: Mark was all those things and more. But then, I am his mother, and memory is colored by love. The urge to prove my evaluation is strong, so here goes.

Statement: He was happy.

Proof: He laughed more than he cried, even at the end. He made us all laugh more than we cried, except at the end.

Statement: He was fun to be around.

Proof: When he was little he would drape a piece of black cloth around his gangly frame and race through the house like Superman. He was silly and loud, and mostly we laughed at him. Sometimes his older brother, Bruce, would shake his head and say, "You've got to do something about Mark!" Being unsure about what I should do, I did nothing, which might have been wrong. Mark stood behind the door when responsibility was delegated, but he had both hands stretched out when it was time for nonsense and fun.

Part of childhood is the memory of kitchen smells. Our children used to breeze in after school through the back door and ask, "When's dinner?" Like most families, we had to struggle to get everyone there at the same time, what with school, games, and meetings, but most nights we managed.

I remember one time I made an apple pie and it was a huge hit. Now, I am not one of those women who cooks meals that children are likely to favor with remarks such as "just like Mom used to make." Occasionally, however, I hit a home run. The apple pie night was one of them. Recognize, now, that this was long before the days of pre-made, refrigerated pie shells, so I sifted, rolled, and filled the whole thing with hand-peeled apples. My pride was as pungent as the aroma. Apparently the memory of that meal remained with Mark for the rest of his life. Funny how those little incremental incidents take on a lasting place in the pantry of our minds.

From that time on, Mark offered a standard joke about it: "Why don't you ever make a really good apple pie like

Mark Clarke at age two.

you used to?" So, every so often I'd offer the treat at the end of the meal. As he grew older, Mark lost his interest in sweets, but not the playful desire to needle my cooking skills. His answer to my offer, be it the symbolic apple pie or cake and ice cream, became "maybe later." Of course, we all knew it was just a courteous reply, and he wouldn't eat dessert. So, in the course of time the word *dessert* was replaced with the phrase, "maybe later," as in, "Will you have some 'maybe later'?"

Funny little family memories.

In his last years I became an avid worker of crossword puzzles. Wordsmithing has always fascinated and entertained me. As the traumas of my life multiplied, I frequently turned to this activity to relieve my mind of hard thinking. As we sat in Mark's hospital room waiting for what we didn't understand, I worked the clues in the daily paper. Mark was, I thought, in and out of consciousness, but mostly out of the wide-awake world. His favorite aunt, Marilynn, was with us biding the time, and we were both seeking answers to a puzzle...the one in hand and the larger one that filled the room.

As I remember, the clue under discussion was something like "a powdery soother." "Hmm...a powdery soother," I mumbled. "Now, what could that be?"

"Let me think," Marilynn mused.

From the hospital bed where Mark rested came his voice: "Talc."

He startled me with his awareness and incisively correct answer. We had thought he was completely out of it. Not so at all. He was very much with us even though we had no sense of his alertness.

This incident stays with me even today, when I feel so separated from Mark because of his death. Those who have lost a loved one will understand what I mean. There are times when the sense of loss almost overwhelms me, and then something happens that whispers a reassurance.

Recently, on an international flight, I was watching a steward move up and down the aisle at his tasks. He was tall, blond, and huskily built. He did not resemble Mark except in coloring. As I was watching him come toward me with the drink cart, our eyes met and he smiled. In that moment, I saw Mark smile at me with the mischief and charm that had been his hallmark. The plunge into memory was as if I had heard "talc" from those white sheets, telling me he was still with me, even if I hadn't the ability to know it.

Statement: He was above average in every way.

Proof: When he was just a youngster he made an offhand

remark to the effect that "Danny's color is orange." Danny was a schoolmate who probably never knew he was orange.

Somewhat taken aback, I asked him what he was talking about. He looked confused and said, "You know, the color around him—it's orange."

That was the first time I realized Mark could see auras.

I made such a fuss about it that he pulled back. Not long afterward, he claimed not to see "the colors" anymore.

He hated being different. Like all kids, he wanted to belong.

Further proof: When he was a teenager, he told me, very seriously, that he knew he would die a young man. I hushed him and said he shouldn't talk like that. He just looked at me as though he were much older and wiser than I. I've never forgotten that moment.

Now, motherlike, I've told of his exceptional qualities, but there were other things. He was irresponsible and lazy. He never denied this. Rather, he would chuckle at his faults. Unfortunately, so would I. Somehow, what was not a laughing matter became a laughing matter.

Mark had an amazing way of justifying actions that the rest of the family criticized, thereby diffusing our accusations of laziness. I remember being at the beach at our much prized house, where worries were meant to evaporate and be replaced with nothing weightier than the latest Anne Rice novel or the question of whether to have scallops or shrimp for dinner. Mark's father was quite industrious and took ownership of Conched Out (beach houses have to have funny names) very seriously. So he painted, repaired, and mowed whenever we were there.

Mark, on the other hand, lounged, read, nibbled, and strolled on the beach, lotion in hand. One time one of us lost patience with his apparent indifference to the work to be done and suggested he might help out. With a surprised look, he replied, "All you have to do is ask," and rose to the occasion both literally and figuratively. That's what I mean when I say we couldn't really stay irritated with him; he was just too good-natured. Still, responsibility sat lightly on him. Sometimes I envy that.

When Mark graduated from college with a degree in biology, his father and I expected him to find a job. But he really wasn't interested in a job that would take him away from the beach house where he had spent his college days, so he quickly found a "temporary" spot where he could ponder the future.

That spot was as a lifeguard at a resort pool. It was a great place, Mark told us, because if it rained at all—even sprinkled—he was relieved of working for the entire day. As you can imagine, it sprinkled frequently. Mark acquired a

Mark Clarke at age 18, posing for his high school graduation photo.

super tan and had lots of time to ponder the future. He eventually worked his way up to a job as a clerk in a Florida T-shirt shop.

This is where he was when our family bubble of happiness began to evaporate. This is where he was in March 1987 when his father Harry's plane crashed. Harry had been flying his own plane home to Asheville from a meeting in Raleigh. The plane took off at 11 P.M. and went down just outside the Asheville airport right after midnight. He was almost home.

It was a sad time, and much of it is dim in my memory. The body has a way of numbing emotions and blanking out awareness of pain.

But I can still see vivid scenes.

In the South, funerals are great gatherings filled with tables heavy with fried chicken, green jellied salad, and overcooked vegetables. One part of a table is devoted to cakes and pies and tiny biscuits stuffed with bright red wedges of ham. Casseroles dripping with melted cheese offer the taste that mothers must have in mind when they say to a finicky child, "Eat! You'll feel better." If the food is plentiful, relatives are even more so. Many cousins and in-laws only come together when a family member "goes on." That euphemism seems to make it easier for us.

So, when Harry died, everyone came home—Mark, from Florida; my daughter Judy from San Diego; Judy's husband, Speedy, who came immediately with my son Bruce and his wife, Diana, from Raleigh; and my daughter Candy, who drove in from Lake Lure, 30 miles away. People poured in, filling our big house with flowers and plants. We all milled about this stage set with people and petals and food, not quite knowing our lines.

Yet, when necessary, the right words quickly rolled off our tongues. Southerners are nothing if not appropriate.

One scene that took place at the time, I never witnessed. I only heard about it, but it is more vivid in my mind's eye than if I had been there myself.

Candy and Mark were standing in the sunporch, looking out the windows at their dad's garden, newly planted with the spring vegetables he would never harvest. Mark began to cry silently, and as his shoulders shook ever so slightly, Candy put her arm around him for comfort.

But there was no comfort for Mark then or for a very long time afterward. The words he spoke revealed an agony much more complex than simple grief.

"My dad's dead," he said. "Now he knows all about me, and he hates me!"

I never knew this until years later, after Mark had finally told me he was gay. Candy knew, of course, and tried to tell him that his dad did not hate him, that he loved him. I hope Mark believed her, because I do.

After Harry died, Mark came home to live with me and to try to figure out what to do with his life. I don't think I was much help, because I couldn't even figure out what to do with my own. So much of our lives had revolved around Harry.

It's hard to explain Harry Clarke. His presence filled any room in which he found himself. This is not to say he was bossy, belligerent, or aggressive. He simply had an inner calm of knowing who he was, what he was about, and who he loved. And those of us left behind were bereft.

I missed the phone ringing and the sound of Harry's voice saying, "OK, doll, I'm leaving the office. Want to go to dinner?" And Mark missed him being there as a bulwark against his insecurities; the biggest one, Harry never knew.

So Mark and I both felt as if we had been relocated to a different planet where we didn't speak the language or know the customs. Even the food tasted different.

Mark had tried marine biology, lifeguarding, data processing, selling T-shirts—what was left? Of course! The theater!

In fairness to Mark, this idea was not as off-the-wall as the time he told me he thought he would go to divinity school because he liked the robes that Episcopal priests wore.

I had been active in theater, teaching and performing for as long as Mark could remember. Mark had even taken part in a children's performance with a good bit of joy and success, so his decision to go into theater seemed to offer possibilities.

Auditions, apprenticeships, and finally graduate school occurred in very rapid succession. He moved back to Florida, and his life changed forever. At a theater where he worked for a time, Mark met "his person."

Mace Graham was a young, talented, handsome man who was the theater's musical director. Very soon after their meeting, Mark called to tell me he was moving in with a young man to share expenses. That sounded unusually practical for Mark, but I was grateful for small favors. The move was accomplished, and they lived together for a year or two before I started to wonder why I never heard about a girlfriend anymore.

It seemed strange to me that on trips home for holidays or visits, Mark found it necessary to call this "roommate" at least once a day. And the calls were long and filled with intimate-sounding conversation—not exactly like a couple of guys kicking the tires.

One day while Mark and I were driving together and he was telling me some story that involved Mace, I finally blurted out, "Mark, are you gay?"

Instead of a direct answer, Mark launched into an expla nation of androgyny that would have made his sociology professor proud. When he finished, I thanked him for the information and repeated my question.

He told me he hadn't decided yet but would tell me when he did.

That scared me, but I've never been one to let a worry go easily. So I pressed on with my questions.

Mark stopped me, and said, "Mom, are you trying to push me into thinking I'm gay?"

Well, of course, that did it. I retreated into my foggy hope that I had misunderstood the whole thing. But I hadn't.

Mark returned to Florida, to Mace, and to his world that was completely separate from us: his conservative, right-wing family.

About three years after his dad's death, Mark called from Florida to tell us he wanted to go to law school. From T-shirts to theater to law school? A gigantic leap for most people, but Mark never even broke his stride. His brother Bruce was a lawyer. His sister Judy was a criminal-defense attorney, and her husband Speedy was also a practicing lawyer. Why not Mark? I was so glad to hear of a reachable focus that I urged him to take the LSAT and apply to schools.

One of my secret longings was that Mark could do it and show he was made of the same stuff that had made his family "successful." And he could have done it. He was accepted to a good law school in California and was doing well, according to his professors.

But something happened in his first year. He began to experience disquieting physical symptoms. He had chronic diarrhea, his gums bled excessively, and he had thrush in his mouth. An alert dentist asked him if he had been tested for HIV. Mark said he hadn't, whereupon the dentist urged him to do so.

The test, of course, was positive. The only person Mark would talk to about this catastrophic diagnosis was Mace, who was still in Florida. Mace must be tested too. HIV is such a capricious predator. It claimed Mark but spared Mace.

Neither Mace nor Mark knew what to do. The doctor who diagnosed Mark told him AIDS was going to kill him but that if he continued in law school, it would kill him faster. So Mark dropped out of the school where he was doing well and actually enjoying it, and returned to Florida and his devoted Mace. He could not bring himself to tell me what was happening to him.

I, of course, was furious. All of my old fears and aggravations about Mark's lack of responsibility and his inability to stick with anything reared up. Once again he was proving his critics correct, those who said I should "do something about Mark."

Well! If this was the way he was going to behave, he'd be on his own—no more checks from me!

It was a year and a half before I learned the truth: that my son was dying and was facing death with more courage and maturity than I could have imagined possible. Where I had perceived weakness and was disappointed, I now recognized strength and was proud.

The way the truth became known to me was accidental. I was planning a visit to West Palm Beach, where Mark worked at Saks Fifth Avenue selling men's clothing. When I phoned him, he made reference to a doctor's appointment, and I remarked that he seemed to be spending a lot of time visiting the doctor for such a young man.

He tried to turn the thought aside, but I wouldn't let him off. I am not stupid. His lecture on androgyny was still in my memory bank. He was still living with Mace, and his days of dating beautiful girls were a thing of the past.

I knew AIDS was an ever-present fear in the gay community, so our phone conversation went like this:

"Mark, are you HIV-positive?"

Silence. And then: "Mom! What a question."

Again: "Mark, are you HIV-positive?" I knew evasion when I heard it.

And again: "Mom, I can't believe you asked me that."

"Then answer me, and I won't ask again. Are you HIV-positive?"

A longer silence this time.

"Yes."

"Are you gay?"

Quickly this time: "Yes." The double whammy.

And now the silence was mine—but brief.

"Well, that's out," I said. "Now, how can we help you get better? We want you to be all right. We love you."

A new fear came into my life that day. The first part was understandable, because it was fear of losing my son.

But the second part was less understandable and felt unnatural: I was afraid of what people would think. I look back now and wonder how that fear could have lived in me, but I know it did, if only briefly.

Someone asked me recently if it would have been harder to accept Mark's homosexuality if he had not been ill. A thoughtful question. If I'd had the luxury of time, it might have taken me longer. But when you face the ultimate reality—that death is imminent—truth is a blinding light. And so it was with me.

Mark lived for two more years after that phone call. They were not easy years. He spent more and more time in and out of the hospital. His towering frame had become stooped, and in his own words, he "tottered like an old man."

Christmas of 1993 came, and Mark knew it would be his last. He was determined to spend that last holiday with his family in North Carolina. Mace couldn't go because of his job, but he knew how much it meant to Mark, so he encouraged him. On December 24, Candy and I met him at the American Airlines gate. He was wearing a sling now, the result of a newly implanted shunt in his shoulder. A shunt is a last resort used to inject the many medications an AIDS patient must take.

Mark smiled, truly glad to see us, as we were him. It was a grim little procession. People stared as we wheeled an obviously very ill young man. I pushed the chair; it was a complete reversal of the way things should have been.

Thus began the saddest Christmas I've ever experienced. There is no point in relating one sad thing after another. There really was nothing happy or good about that time except that we were together.

When Mark left to return to Florida, Mace took him back to the hospital, where something truly remarkable occurred. The doctor put Mark on an intravenous nutrition program that improved his condition beyond all expectations. He was able to go home, continuing this treatment. He gained weight, his spirits rose, and we began to hope. I returned to my teaching commitment in San Diego, and our skies were brightened.

Just as I was completing my stay in the West, Mace called and said things had taken a bad turn, and that I should come back quickly. I went straight to the hospital from the airport, my bags flapping from my shoulders. I was familiar with the AIDS wing and knew where Mark's room probably was.

As I turned down his hall, I saw a nurse I recognized standing outside of a room. She saw me and waved me on as though to hurry. My breath left me, and I thought, *He's gone. Oh, please, God, don't let him be gone.*

As I turned into that white room, my emotional distress was so strong that I felt surrounded by loud, discordant sounds. But the moment I entered the room, I stopped still, and silence swept all of the clamor of my emotions away.

There before me lay my youngest child, his long frame almost hanging off the foot of the bed, even with the extension the hospital had provided. He was sleeping the sleep of the exhausted and the dying.

Seated in a chair next to this misshapen bed was Mace, his devoted companion. The chair faced Mark, and Mace too was sleeping, exhaustion and grief across his face. The sight that stays in my memory is of their two hands clasped together.

That moment was the turning point in my understanding of a love and devotion that had always mystified—and, perhaps, repulsed—me. There, in that room, where Mark would breathe his last breath, I stood and prayed silently: *Oh, Lord, please let me remember this. How could I have ever doubted this love, this devotion?*

So far, this prayer has been answered, and I have never doubted it since.

Mark did not die that day. He lived a few more weeks. In a way, I think he was spared a great deal because his last diagnosis was toxoplasmosis. "Toxo," as the doctors call it, can cause blindness, brain damage, and a host of terrible manifestations. Fortunately, Mark was excused from these experiences.

I had been in Florida with Mark for a while when I decided to go back to Raleigh and get my situation in order. It was March, and of course, no matter what's happening in your life, you have to pay your taxes, so I had to go home to do that. I had to arrange for the cat to be put in the kennel. I packed up my knitting and my crossword books and was prepared to go back to Florida.

I had come back up to North Carolina on a Friday and was to return to Florida on Monday. That Saturday, my daughters, Candy and Judy, went down to be with Mace and Mark so that someone from the family would be there for the weekend.

Mark had a little dog named Meeper, a Japanese Chin that weighed maybe four pounds. Mark was so big, and Meeper was so small, and they loved each other so. Hospitals frown upon dogs visiting patients, so that week-end, Candy and Judy brought Meeper to the hospital, hoping that Mark could come out in the wheelchair to see him. They got their towering brother into his undersize wheel-chair, attached his IVs, tucked his feet under the blanket, and wheeled him outside.

By this time, Mark had had a stroke, and half of his face had fallen. He was extremely weak. The girls got him out-side, where he drew stares from nurses, other patients, and their visitors. He was obviously in bad shape. Candy and Judy brought in Meeper and placed him in Mark's lap, and Mark leaned down and petted him, out in the clean air, without the smell of antiseptics or medicine and without the rustle of emergencies.

It was a comfort, two sisters visiting their brother. Candy, blond and 12 years Mark's senior, gazed at her brother with the maternal look she'd had for him all his life. Judy, lanky and brunette, kept the laughs going. To Judy, 10 years older than Mark, her little brother could do no wrong. I think she would have sold her soul if it would have saved him.

Candy and Judy took pictures of their brother. After a while they took him back to his room and the dog back to the house, got on their different airplanes, and flew back to their jobs. The next day, I arrived.

Something made me not unpack. Something made me go to the hospital first. So I arrived there at about 10 in the morning, my bags lying in the corner, and stayed for lunch. Mace and I talked about what the weekend had been like, how Mark was feeling. I kept putting off going to my hotel room. Finally, I said to Mace, "I think I'll wait until after dinner, and then I'll go over and you can stay while I get settled in and I'll come back. But I'll wait until Mark's had dinner."

So they brought in his dinner: Thai chicken. I've only eaten that dish once since then. Mark was in the bed and Mace was sitting and watching television, and I fed Mark, just as I did when he was a baby.

I cut up the chicken and gave him a piece as he rolled over toward me—he still had a good appetite—and he ate it. And he had his favorite drink, Mountain Dew, with one of those crooked straws you can bend. He had a bite and then a sip. And he rested a minute in between.

At one point he leaned toward me, and I leaned toward him. He went into a fetal position, and his body began to shake, and he spewed blood from his mouth and convulsed, his eyes rolling back in his head. I screamed, and Mace called for help. They coded it and the cart came, and it was just like television.

I have this memory of bells clanging, but I probably imagined that.

They came in, around six of them, all around a cart, telling me to move out of the way, and they put up a sign on the wall that said KEEP BACK! DANGER OF CONVULSIONS. They strapped him down, they confined him, and they jabbed him full of medicine.

I found myself at Mark's feet—remember, he was 6 feet 7 inches tall—and I had his feet in my hands and I was rubbing them. I heard myself singing. I heard my voice singing this song—the song I sang to all of my children.

Rock-a-bye and don't you cry,
Rock-a-bye, little Mark.
I'll buy you a pretty gold horse
To ride all around your pasture

I rubbed his feet and sang this baby song. All of a sudden I realized, as we do at times like this, the irony and ridiculousness of my singing that song when my son was in his death throes. And I stopped because it wasn't appropriate, and I stepped back.

One of the nurses at Mark's head looked up at me and shouted, "Keep singing!"

So I went back to singing and rubbing his feet. I realized later that you don't know what a patient in that condition can hear, and if there was any chance that I comforted him, it was worth doing.

Mark was never the same after that. He talked for the whole evening—and as fast as he could. I could understand the words, but they didn't make sense. He just strung names and words together like mismatched beads on a string that had no end. We would sometimes catch a phrase, but we wouldn't know what he meant. Mace and I just stood there, rubbing Mark's hands, saying, "Rest, Mark."

The next day, one of his doctors came in and called us into the hall. "He's not going to last past this afternoon," he said.

Doctors have a way of saying the most God-awful things as if they're saying, "We're going to have tea at 3." And of course, they have to, because otherwise everyone would stay in a state of absolute capsizing all the time. I understand that.

Mark had two primary physicians: Dr. Weiwora and Dr. Rosada. Dr. Weiwora was a teddy bear of a man, a bit rotund with an easy manner. He was fatherly toward Mark, who loved him. During that awful Christmas visit in Raleigh, I realized how very dependent Mark was on this man. He called him almost every day with his problems, and Dr. Weiwora always eased his immediate worries. Of course, this was always long distance, which made me even more aware of the magical kindness that dear man extended.

Dr. Rosada was very different, but just as essential and caring to Mark. He had a bit of a Spanish accent and was much smaller than Dr. Weiwora. He was the one with us in those final days. It was he who told us Mark would not last past the afternoon. Gently, with his soft brown eyes saying

Mace Graham with Mark Clarke just after Mark's diagnosis in 1990.

what his voice could not utter, he helped us accept the last page of Mark's life.

Dr. Rosada looked at us and said, "I can put him on the morphine drip with your permission." I didn't know what a morphine drip was. And I looked at Mace, because I recognized, by that time, the strength and reality of their relationship. If it had been my son and his wife, I would have turned to the wife and said, "What do you want to do?" Because I would think that was the right choice, the right person.

Mace looked at me, and he was so young then in my eyes. I saw the terror in his face. "I don't know," he said. "What do you think?"

"I'll do whatever you want to do. But I think we should put him on the drip, because he's obviously in such distress. He's not himself."

Mark feared two things most: losing his looks and losing his mind. Now he was doing both. Mark had told Mace to "let me go if I reach that point."

The doctor put Mark on the drip and repeated that he wouldn't last past that afternoon. I went to the phone and called Candy and Judy and Bruce and told them Mark was dying and probably would not last through the day.

Neither of Mark's doctors returned to that vigil room. At the time, I kept thinking that the doctor would come soon. Later I realized that the doctor would not come soon because his work was over. It was left to us to close the door. In retrospect, I think that men like these doctors can only bear so much agony in their chosen work. They had both cared for Mark, physically and lovingly, over several years' time. They liked him. Watching him die was their pain as well as ours. And they had to watch patients die over and over. No wonder they had to spare themselves the last moments.

So we were left with the nurses. Saints they were. They cared for us, the family, as well as for Mark. They joked and laughed with him till he could no longer play his part. One wept with us at the end.

Mark's brother and sisters had only recently been at his bedside. They all had jobs in far corners of the country. Candy is a high school biology teacher in Skyland, N.C.; Judy is a well-known federal defender based in Spokane, Wash.; and Bruce is a labor lawyer in Raleigh.

Mark's illness had certainly ebbed and flowed: There were times when he suffered from extreme nausea and headaches. Other times it was neuropathy, when he lost the feeling in his feet and needed help to walk. And at the disease's very worst, he convulsed.

So I think at the moment the other children felt I was being overly fearful. I also think they simply could not believe their kid brother would die. Judy even said, "We were just there. He looked so much better. Really, it's not going to happen yet. He's better."

Bruce had been to the hospital and bought Mark a comfortable recliner to sit in after he went home. I remember how much it meant to Mark that his brother came. He said, "Bruce is just like Dad." He could pay him no higher compliment. And I don't think Bruce could believe that his brother would not go home.

Candy said, "Call me back if you really think it's that bad."

I called her back and said, "I really think it's that bad." Candy and Marilynn, my sister-in-law, caught a plane and arrived in time to be there for Mark—and for me.

I remember that long, awful night. I had gone for almost two days without sleep. And when awful things are happening, your body gives out; I couldn't stand it much longer. Literally, I couldn't stand up—and Mace couldn't either.

The nurses were so kind. They told me to lie down, and I was asleep before my head hit the pillow. Not long after that, somebody shook me and said, "You need to come back now."

I got up and went back to Mark's room, and Mace was there. He'd had his rest too. So I did the stupidest thing: I went and ate breakfast because that was an ordinary, understandable thing to do. I went downstairs and had my cereal and French toast. And my son was upstairs dying in bed. My mother had always said, "Eat. You'll feel better." I didn't.

I went back up to Mark's room at about quarter to 10. And that's when the nurse took Mark's vitals. I saw tears running down her cheeks when she looked up at me and nodded.

Was I sad? Of course I was sad. That's a given. But I also felt a sense of release. Just the day before, I'd stood at his window and prayed: *Lord, take him.* So yes, certainly, I felt relief for Mark.

Mostly, I felt an incredible sense of failure. In some distorted way, I believed Mark's death was my fault. Mothers feel the need to be omnipotent and omnipresent. I felt very…singular…and full of failure. I had failed the thing that mattered most: caring for my child.

But I know that's irrational because we raise our children giving them the greatest gift of all: We let them go.

It was March 9, 1994, exactly seven years after Harry had died in that plane crash. Mark's death felt almost as things did when Harry died: a turning point in the script of my life that I had to play out. At that time, I knew I would get through it. Because you do.

Of course, the family came immediately. The necessary arrangements and phone calls were made. I remember one of those calls especially. After my friend on the other end of the line expressed her sorrow, she said, "Patsy, what do you want us to tell people?"

"Tell them the truth," I answered. "He was a gay man who died of AIDS."

The double whammy.

During the in-between days before the first memorial services (one in Florida, one in North Carolina), we did the ordinary things mourners do. One of them was to pick up the roll of snapshots that Candy and Judy had taken of Mark and Meeper that last weekend.

Judy and Candy looked at those pictures together. I

think I had seen Mark with more realism than they had. I don't know why. But both of the girls looked at those pictures, and it was very clear—it couldn't be mistaken—this was a dying man. You couldn't have wished for him to live any longer.

"I thought he was so much better," Judy said. "How could I have thought that?"

It made me realize that so often our eyes see only what we will them to see.

I'm glad we had those pictures, as ugly as they are, because they made us realize it was time for Mark to leave this world.

As the door to Mark's life was closing, a different door in my life opened, one that showed me an understanding I had not dreamed possible.

Chapter Two

MARK VAUGHN, BY HIS MOTHER

I never in my life thought I would be able to give any-one a shot—much less one of my children, whom I love like my soul.

I figured we had many good doctors, and they could take care of it. But when I finally faced the fact that the doctors were not going to be able to keep my oldest, my first son, in the hospital for his last days—and that those days could stretch out a lot longer than any of us ever realized—I knew I'd have to get over my fear of needles.

I just didn't want to hurt him.

When Mark came home from Atlanta, he was in pretty bad shape. We hired round-the-clock licensed practical nurses. And I thought, these people know how to give shots. Why can't they do it? Surely they can do it, and then Mark will be safe because they'll give him the shot and they'll know the right place and they won't hurt him.

I asked one nurse to do it, and she said, "Well, you know, Ms. Vaughn, I'm not supposed to do this because I'm not licensed to give shots in a home. But you're such a nice woman that I'll do it. We just won't tell anybody."

I thought I was off the hook for a while. But somehow word got back that the nurse was giving the shots instead of me, so the home-care agency called and said, "Ms. Vaughn, if you keep doing this, we won't be able to provide you with services. We're sorry, but things like this endanger our license, and we can't do it."

Well. I wanted to do the right thing. I really didn't want to get anyone in trouble, so I thought, *I can do this. I can do this.*

And I realized that we can always do what we have to. So I practiced with an orange and a grapefruit, and I learned how to give a shot. Before it was all over, I was giving Mark Vaughn 16 shots a day. I never even batted an eye at giving him a shot there at the last part, even in the middle of the night. I wanted to be able to give him everything I could.

He really was so brave. When he was diagnosed in October 1987, he weighed about 210 pounds, was broad-shouldered, and looked like an "all-American boy."

By the end, almost three years later, Mark's weight had dropped to less than 100 pounds. His face was hollow, his limbs bony. He had lost his sight. He had lost control of his bodily functions. He became paralyzed. He was essentially dead, but his body plugged on. He was 34 years old.

I realized that death was imminent and that I had to make funeral arrangements. This wasn't something I needed to wait to do until he died. I needed to do it immediately.

So I called the funeral home. We had lived in Raleigh,

N.C., for a long time. My late husband, Earl, had been a judge on the state court of appeals and, up until his death, served on the North Carolina Supreme Court. We were respected, not unknown, and we had always done the best we could by our family.

I called the most prominent funeral home in town—they had directed Earl's service three years before—and told them I needed to make arrangements for my dying son. I thought it was all straightened out, that they would take care of everything. So I put it out of my mind.

It was approaching Mother's Day, right around May 15, 1990, such a rejuvenating time in Raleigh. Life truly bursts open. Dogwoods, with their cottony white blossoms, make the yards and woods look as if they are covered in snow. Azaleas are luscious pink or fuchsia, the greenery is bright and new, and every breath draws the smell of roses and freshly cut grass.

Inside my house, though, we were waiting for death.

A Catholic priest came by every day. Father Jeffrey Ingham was the parish priest of a friend of mine, and she asked me one day if it would be all right if Father Ingham came to say a blessing for Mark. I figured we needed all the blessings we could get and said, "Yes, please."

I'm not Catholic. None of my children were raised Catholic, but a Catholic priest came.

Father Ingham was a tall, thin, balding man with the kindest face and warmest blue eyes I had ever seen. Gentle, urbane, witty, intellectual, thoughtful, he was a joy to have around. He is also, to me, the living example of Christian love and concern. He never spoke of loving the sinner but hating the sin.

Tentatively, Father Ingham began visiting Mark up in

Mark Vaughn, age 29, at the swearing-in reception for his father at the North Carolina Supreme Court Jan. 2, 1985.

his room, since Mark was already bedridden. At first he came a few days a week. Then, as Mark's condition worsened, he came every day. He asked me if it was it all right. Was it all right? I am eternally grateful to that man for coming because the minister of my very own church had to be prodded into coming to see Mark at the end.

That was when I realized how the stigma of having an undesirable disease can change a lot of minds.

I didn't want Mark to feel rejected by the church, so I was grateful to Father Ingham for his loving care, especially the night he administered the last rites.

The night Mark died, we knew he was very low. He hardly responded to questions and seemed far away. A young woman sent by the nursing agency sat with Mark while I tried to get a little rest, but I still got up at 4 A.M. to give him his shot.

I always worried about that 4 A.M. shot. Did I give him too much? Was it too strong? Did it push him over the edge? And yet my rational mind said no. I know I gave him exactly what he was supposed to have and nothing more.

I went back to bed, and I told the young woman before I went, "If there's any change, you get me up." I could hardly stand, I was so tired. I got back into bed, and I went right back to sleep.

The next thing I remember was that girl standing by the side of my bed. It wasn't even really morning, but dawn was starting. I could feel little glimmers of light coming in through the blinds.

"Ms. Vaughn? Ms. Vaughn? I'm going now. Good-bye."

I got up and said, "Well, I'm getting right up." But she was already out the door.

Somehow I knew things weren't right.

I ran up those stairs and Mark was gone. I hadn't been there by his side. He went alone.

I stood there a little while and realized why the girl had left. She was afraid. She had probably fallen asleep, woken up, saw that Mark was dead, and couldn't deal with it. I was outraged and hurt by this, but in the days that followed, I never called the agency to complain. How much more pain could I go through?

I walked downstairs, in that house where they all grew up: Mark, John, Stuart, and Rose. And I was alone.

I went to the phone and called them all. And I thought, *Now, what is it that I do? What is the next thing that I do?* I remembered that I had to call the funeral home, glad I had all that arranged. The number was close by since I kept it by the phone in case I had to call immediately. I dialed the number. An unfamiliar voice answered.

"This is Mrs. Earl Vaughn. My son Mark just died. I made the arrangements with you to come and get him... The AIDS finally took him."

The voice said, "AIDS?"

"Well, yes. AIDS."

"I'm so sorry, Mrs. Vaughn. There must have been some kind of misunderstanding. This funeral home doesn't handle deaths by AIDS."

I almost didn't know how to answer. I only knew to be polite.

"I'm sorry, I must have misunderstood. Forgive me, and I thank you."

I hung up the phone, and thought, I've lived in Chapel Hill all my growing-up years. I can call a funeral home in Chapel Hill. I did, and a voice said, "Why, certainly, Mrs. Vaughn. We'll be glad to help you. We'll be right over. You don't have to do another thing."

※ ※ ※

Mark, unknowingly, had been a great teacher. As he lay in his childhood room upstairs for 18 months, we talked. We talked about everything: what his life was really like while he was living in Atlanta, which was as far away as possible from us—but still in the South. We talked about his friends and his failure to find an honest-to-goodness partner.

He told me he had known since he was very young that he was different from the other boys in his class. Of course, we all had been aware that there was something different, but we never discussed it or gave it a name.

As the first child born into a tight circle of young married couples, there was a lot expected of Mark Vaughn, and he delivered.

He was a beautiful baby, with blond ringlets around his head and pink skin—the softest, most beautiful skin his mother had ever seen. Like silk. He was a good baby who ate well, slept long, and behaved. He seemed to want to make people happy.

But as he grew older, I noticed how hard he worked to please others, almost to the point of putting himself out of time, money, and his own opportunities. He bent over backward for teachers, friends of the family—even *their* friends. It seemed he felt he had to work to make people love him because he knew one reason why they might not.

He was afraid he wasn't good enough for the straight world. He hoped he could make a place in people's hearts if only he could please them. So he showered them with gifts and kindness. For my 20th wedding anniversary with Earl, for example, he planned a surprise party and invited all our friends. During his last Christmas, he gave me a gold watch, which fell off my wrist a year or so after he died. I found it but never wore it again. I'm afraid of losing it again (and for good).

As Mark grew older, he drifted from boys in his age group toward the girls—especially one named Patty Clarke. He could have spent every waking moment with her, not because she was a girl but because they enjoyed the same things: talking endlessly on the phone, making plans. If a friend came over for dinner, it was Patty. Their closeness never flagged, even as Mark came closer to death.

All four of the children were loving and devoted to us and to one another, but Mark always seemed to want to get closer. He wrote the most beautiful cards on special occasions. Presents for everyone were of greatest importance. He always lavished care and attention on his baby sister Rose. That last Christmas, he gave Rose copper molds shaped like the sun, moon, and stars, saying he was sorry he couldn't give her the real things.

Even as a little boy, Mark was different from his two younger brothers, which disturbed his father. The summer following the sixth grade, his father had enrolled him in Hargrave Military Academy in Chatham, Va. My husband, Earl, wanted to "straighten out" what he perceived to be laziness because of Mark's disinterest in sports and a general feeling that, yes, something was not quite the way he wanted it to be.

The experience at Hargrave was disastrous and traumatic for Mark. I have never read such sad letters, begging us to please come and bring him home. He was truly pathetic and never would have taken to that place. His father made him stay the entire summer, but even he could not force more of that treatment on the child, and we never sent him back.

When Mark was 8 years old, his father took him to the softball field behind the local junior high, where the YMCA was starting its spring softball season. The coach called all the boys onto the field, talked to them, and then announced they would begin by running for a while around the edge of the diamond. Mark sat on the bench, refusing to run.

His father, the judge, was insistent, then firm toward his son. "Don't you want to try?" he said. "At least try, Mark." Mark refused to move.

The judge then roared with anger, "Get out there!"

But Mark would not run. Nothing could have moved him from that bench.

Whatever he wasn't in his father's eyes was put aside

when Mark entered high school and got involved in the theater department. He had a deep, resonant baritone voice that rose easily from his tall, broad-shouldered body. For him, the high point of high school came when he appeared in *Brigadoon*. Never had he had so much fun at school, which had been hard for him to adjust to in several ways. Many of the students who participated in that play would become lifelong friends of his, and all of them had extraordinary talents. Two girls, his best friends, went on to perform on Broadway. Another has spent the last 25 years as an entertainer and pianist in Atlanta.

Brigadoon was a great success. Mark loved having the group over to our house for parties, and an enduring love and vocation were born. Until his illness, he participated in all kinds of productions wherever he found himself. He sang at his brother's wedding. He traveled to plays, loving to go to New York, especially to see his friends perform on Broadway.

It was this interest that led him to major in communications at North Carolina State University. While there, he worked part-time at a local TV station and also at the university's TV station. He took part in plays produced by various theater companies on campus, as well as the Raleigh Little Theater. He was a happy and devoted member of the men's glee club and the music fraternity.

Mark auditioned and was accepted into the summer program at the North Carolina School for the Arts in Winston-Salem, and he also performed for two summers at the Farm House, a large, old Victorian inn located in the "high country" town of Blowing Rock, N.C. Since winters are so long and rigorous up there, performances took place only in the summer.

The Farm House was a unique venue for college students who were aspiring singers, dancers, musicians, and actors. Not only did these two dozen or so kids wait tables, but they also put on miniproductions from popular musicals and the classics, and they sang and danced for the guests after dinner every night in the Parlor.

It was hard work for an entire summer, but the most difficult part was getting accepted there the previous winter. The Farm House required tapes of the students' work and recommendations from teachers and tutors, and students came from all over the country to work there. Once they arrived, though, it was all worth it: Lifetime friendships were formed amid amazing singing and acting.

Mark was delighted to work there for two college summers, and several times my husband and I and one or two of the other children journeyed up to stay in the antique-filled rooms, soak in the cool air and 100-mile views, and delight in Mark's performances.

The young actors rotated working in Parlor productions, but when we were visiting, Mark always made it onto the stage. Each night the performing group split the tips from the Parlor. Whenever we were there, Mark put forth his best effort, and by evening's end, the tall silk hat on the stand by the door would be overflowing with bills.

Mark would introduce us with a flourish and, as always, dedicate songs to us. The most beautiful and touching, and the one that stays with me today, is the one he dedicated to his baby sister, Rose: "The Rose," made famous by Bette Midler.

Today the song haunts me, and the words have taken on a deeper and more spiritual meaning. I think I want it read—or better, sung—at my funeral. It is forever tied up with my fondest, dearest memories of my happy, enthusiastic, ebullient Mark. Its bittersweet words are always with me: It's the one who won't be taken who cannot seem to give / And the soul afraid of dying that never learns to live.

And I might add: *And the one who is afraid of thinking who will never learn nor understand.*

Ultimately, Mark's involvement in the theater led him to what would be a tragically short-lived career as a producer for a TV station in Atlanta. There, he loved the work and being around the real "stars" and newspeople.

While working at WAGA in Atlanta, he met and became friends with Virginia Gunn, the station's star personality and human-interest newsperson. She was and is beautiful, vivacious, talented, and, above all, a lover of people. She loved Mark throughout his years there and did many kind things for him. Later her connection would help me deal with the end of Mark's life.

It's funny how clearly I remember the beginning of the end, when the time since has been such a blur. It all started in colors.

It was October 1987. The air was crisp and clear, and leaves blanketed the ground in crimson and gold. I was doing my needlepoint, watching Dan Rather deliver the news. The fireplace was crackling a warm orange.

It had been about 18 months since Earl had died of lung cancer, and Mark was home helping me get through this time. I was separating yarn when he walked in. Scarlet.

"Mama," he said. "I have something to tell you."

I set the yarn in my lap and waited.

"Mama, it's almost a sure thing that I have AIDS. I've seen Dr. Page, and the results will be in tomorrow. Will you be with me when he tells me?"

I didn't cry. He didn't cry. I was just in shock as Mark told me of his symptoms: weight loss and thrush. I was devastated. And scared.

I grasp on to little things from this point on, moments that I can hold and focus on amid the hurricane of the next year or so.

I remember being in the doctor's office, and how my skin went cold and my stomach turned to steel as I recalled a line I had read in *Newsweek:* "After being diagnosed with AIDS, the patient has approximately one year to live." That was a year before when I'd read that, and I'd thought, *What a terrible thing. I wonder if that will ever affect me.*

The diagnosis was confirmed, and on that day, it seemed, Mark began to die. There were rises in the journey: AZT, Mark's occasional and brief rallies. But then the day came when he was bedridden in the same room he grew up in. He stayed there for 18 months.

I watched as Mark became blind, incontinent, and paralyzed. I was his constant nurse. Mark used to apologize for the "trouble" he was causing me. One weekend he even had a friend stay with him so I could get away to my favorite spot in the mountains for a respite from the constant care he needed.

I watched Mark sleep and thought about how I knew he was gay, how I feared he would die, and, like anyone, worried how the family would be treated once the stigma of AIDS set in.

I had grown up in the Methodist Church and sang in the choir the song that claimed that God's children, "Black and yellow, brown and white / They are precious in his sight." In the worst days of Mark's short life, I sat in his room and wondered if that song could ever include God's gay sons and daughters.

The Vaughn family in the summer of 1967. Back row: John (age 9), Mark (age 12), and Stuart (age 7). Front row: Eloise, Earl, and Rose (age 3).

I knew that even if the song didn't include them, God did. Bruce Stanley, an associate pastor, and Vernon Tyson, a retired minister, offered comfort and kindness to us. Still, the minister of my church did not visit or call during my darkest days, except for the two times I begged him to come over. And I did beg. I wanted Mark to feel the comfort and acceptance of the church in which he was raised.

In the end, though, it was that Catholic priest who became a genuine friend, calling every day for months, even administering the sacraments to Mark.

As those last months dragged by, my formerly 210-pound, 6-foot-1 son appeared almost skeletal. Nurses came around the clock. His friends came from New York, Atlanta, and Washington, D.C., to visit with him.

As we talked during those last painful months, he told

me what so many gay friends have told me since: that no one would ever choose to be gay. Life was hard enough without having to hide his true self, without having to put up with the slurs and even threats to his own safety.

Mark never conveyed this, but one gay friend said to me later, "I would have cut off my right arm when I was younger—before I finally accepted who I really am—if I could have stopped being gay."

Many of my gay and lesbian friends have also told me that once they gain self-confidence and a sense of who they really are, they love being themselves and enjoy life to its fullest. It takes love and support for one to achieve this, though. That's why it is so important that the straight world learn that gay people are normal just as they are. We are not being thoughtful when we denigrate, marginalize, or even demonize people who are different from us.

Mark explained that he was always afraid people would find out he was gay and that it would hurt his father's career as a judge. He felt surer and safer at home now that, sadly, his father was gone.

Although we lived in a conservative area, I trusted and knew, even at the beginning, that my friends would not turn away—and they didn't.

Mark had not been a regular churchgoer, but I did not want him to think that the church could turn its back on him now during this terrible sickness. So I asked my minister to come to see us at my home. I had been a devoted member and regular churchgoer all my life and did not think it could ever see anything about Mark that was not pure compassion, love, and beauty.

The Methodist Book of Discipline states that homosexuality is incompatible with Christian teaching. Was that why, I wondered, the minister only came twice during those wretched 18 months? Was that why he offered communion just once?

The young assistant minister came once to meet me in the emergency room at Duke Hospital during one of our many crises. The Rev. Jimmy Creech, who at that time did not have a church to pastor because of his great compassion for gay people (he later was removed from his church in Nebraska for performing a commitment ceremony for two lesbians), also came with communion.

The thing that astounds me to this day, though, was the love and devotion of Father Ingham. He had the largest Catholic church and school in Raleigh, yet what he did still puts me in awe of what true love and compassion can be and do. I was surprised that this priest, a stranger to me, was willing to get involved with an AIDS patient.

Mark was impressed with him; he appreciated the personal attention from such a kind man. I did not know it then, but this man of the church would make a profound difference in our lives for the remainder of Mark's life.

In those days the door was never locked, and the front hall light was always on, so nurses and friends could always see themselves in and out. Father Ingham was there every day.

I later learned that Father Ingham had talked Mark out of suicide. My family can never repay or forget his ministry to us. Finally there was someone with authority from the church to answer Mark's questions: "Am I going to hell? What is it like to die?"

There is a song that has played background music to me for years now. Written by Mark's close friend, Christian Benschop Davenport, it was sung at his funeral, and has since been recorded by another friend who is a professional musician.

Bittersweet and lovely, it is called "Let It Be the Song."

If I cannot stay with you forever
And the time comes that I must be moving on
Tell me what will it be that you will have of me
That will linger when I'm gone?
Let it be the song
Let it be the smile
Let it be the joy that lingers for a while
Let it be the good times and laughter
That will echo ever after
Let it be the love you dwell upon
There are times when the load is just too heavy
And we rage against the way the world is made
And we wonder why it should be
Letting go can bring such agony
And we wonder if the path is worth the pain
Let it go and let it be the song
Let it be the smile
Let it be the joy that lingers for a while
Let it be the good times and laughter
That will echo ever after
Let it be the song
Let the melody play on

Mark was buried next to his father in the country churchyard by the side of the small Methodist church where I had sung the song about God's children. The spring violets dotted the shroud of green. Purple and green.

At first, right after Mark's death, I could not see how the colors of my life would change again and again. But they had already started without my realizing it. And that would bring me great satisfaction and a deep sense of peace.

Chapter Three

HOW I LEARNED TO LOVE LIBERALS

Harry Clarke had our kitchen table custom-made so that it would be large enough to accommodate our whole family on a regular and comfortable basis. He wanted it to be the place where he and I, our four children, and my mother and father could gather to be nurtured both physically and intellectually, a place where we feasted on Boston cream pie and the news of the day with equal relish.

This round oak table became the hub of our lives, around which so many of our family's notable events occurred. Thomas "Speedy" Rice asked for Judy's hand in marriage at that table. Harry always swore he never gave permission, rather that he just stood up and went to bed. I, on the other hand, was so excited that I ran to the phone and called the wedding photographer—the difference between men and women.

This is the same round table where we all gathered on

Sundays for our weekly pot-roast dinner. It was the same round table where we all sat in silence upon our return from the memorial services for both my mother and my father...and for Harry.

Political discussions abounded at that table. We subscribed to conservative publications such as *Human Events* and *The Dan Smoot Report* and hosted John Birch meetings in our living room. We worked on petitions to impeach Supreme Court justice Earl Warren. I never knew why we wanted to impeach him. I only knew I wanted to do the "right" thing.

Even then it seemed a bit extreme, like seeing Communists under the bed.

I was encouraged to believe that Frank Porter Graham, then-president of the University of North Carolina, was undermining its educational structure. Graham ran for the U.S. Senate against Willis Smith, and lost his bid after one of the most vitriolic campaigns in the history of the state.

In 1972 our daughters excused themselves from that kitchen table and voted for George McGovern. When I found out, it took me weeks to get over the shock. I never even told Harry.

We were "consistent conservatives." We didn't believe in welfare because "people should take care of themselves." That's such a simple philosophy, no gray areas, an "easy" solution. Ayn Rand was a guiding light.

In reality it was a harsh, unbending way of thinking, but it was the one I grew up with and married into.

I was born in 1929, the year the Great Depression began. My father was the manager of the movie theater in Adams, Mass. I loved the cold, snowy winters and the library. Books are still an endless source of enjoyment for me. We moved to Asheville, N.C., when I was a teenager, and I was able to study theater arts in high school. From that time on, I have loved and worked in (in one way or another) the theater.

In June 1949, while attending summer school at Furman University in Greenville, S.C., I met Harry Clarke, a GI student who was very bright and in a hurry to finish his schooling so he could get started with his life. He was tall— 6 foot 2—very slender and blond, and he asked the most intelligent questions in our psychology class. To this day, I believe him to be the smartest, most interesting man I have ever known. Ours was a real whirlwind courtship. We eloped six weeks after we met, and we were still happily together almost 38 years later when Harry's plane went down near the Asheville airport.

All those years, I maintained the same views as those around me: my parents, and then Harry. Accepting homosexuality was out of the question. It was aberrant behavior, something that could be corrected. We thought about it, and then it was gone; it would never touch our lives, so why fret about it?

The only connection I had—knowingly—with gay people was in the theater. I liked them but didn't care to consider what went on in their lives.

Then, in 1993, the summer before Mark died, there I was again at that table, which had been transported to our house at the beach. Mace sat at my left and Mark to my right. I was getting used to thinking of them as a couple. We were talking about the gay rights group ACT UP and some big to-do it was putting on in New York. I was struggling to understand a miasma of new thoughts but still clung to many of the old familiar ones.

"It seems to me that 'those people' are really hurting the cause," I said. "They look so ridiculous in those outfits, flaunting themselves."

Instead of the agreement I expected from my son and his partner, they both grew silent. I felt like both were pulling away from me. Their eyes almost rebuked me, and I became very defensive.

"Well, can't you can see how it looks to people like me?"

They remained silent. Finally, in exasperation, I fumed at them, "Now, don't shut me out. I'm on your side, remember?"

Mace just shook his head and said, "You don't understand."

He was right. I didn't understand, and at that point I wasn't sure I wanted to. It was too hard and painful to reexamine beliefs I had held for so long...beliefs that were so comfortable because they were shared by most of my world.

When I look back on that small moment in time, I realize how much my thinking has changed. I still think public displays of a certain sort are not to my taste, but I have come to believe that sometimes zealotry is necessary to create sensitivity.

I remember that night years later during the MAJIC campaign, in a gay bar, when Eloise and I met a lawyer, a stockbroker, and an older woman—all of them gay. It startled me. It wasn't what I expected; it was better. These were good people who understood my struggle and believed in what I was doing. They didn't talk about things I would resent, and they didn't embarrass me.

My son Mark had probably been to bars like this. He had probably met friends, felt at ease and more at home in places like this than he did around the revered Clarke kitchen table.

It was only after Mark had acknowledged his homo-sexuality and HIV status that I knew the agony he had experienced in hiding; how he had spent his life sitting at the dinner table, hungering for acceptance from his own family.

When I became a "recovered Republican," I suddenly felt like I was free. I didn't have to take these great, hard-line, rigid positions about things. I didn't have to say, "Well, absolutely not!" or "Of course, everyone knows!" I could simply say, "Hmm. Well, maybe so. I'll think about that."

There was a sense of freeing up, and I remember saying to someone, "When you're a liberal, you don't have to be against everything. You can be for some things, or you can even consider being for some things. Whereas, when I was a conservative, I had to know exactly where I stood. I had to be consistent."

But I've discovered that human beings are not consistent.

Patsy, Harry, and Mark Clarke in the summer of 1980 during a trip to Cape Cod.

There's a wonderful quote from Emerson: "A foolish consistency is the hobgoblin of little minds."

Tossing off the bonds of conservatism was incredibly freeing for me. The restraints of conservatism meant that if I wanted to fit in, I couldn't express displeasure with some beliefs. I knew what was expected of me.

The place where I began to break out was back in Asheville, when Harry and Mark were still alive. My world was still very much intact. I knew what I was supposed to think.

Harry and I attended a dinner party with some very conservative people, and I thought I knew how to act. We were sitting there at the table, and one of the issues in our town at that time was book censorship in libraries and whether *The Catcher in the Rye* should be allowed. The woman sitting across from me was explaining why book censorship was necessary. She also said we needed to support a certain woman who was running for county commissioner because she was in favor of book censorship and would know what was right for our children to read. We had to guard these young minds, she said.

I couldn't believe what I was hearing, so I spoke up. "I don't approve of book censorship."

"Then you'd be in favor of pornography being available to children," she said.

I thought about that, and I realized it was a trap.

"Yes," I said, calling her bluff. "I guess I would. Just so I could protect all the other books."

I remember her sitting back and looking at me. She had what we would call an "industrial" hairdo, all poufed up, and her lipstick was on just right and she was just...fixed. She was broad-breasted, and she puffed herself out and said, "You really aren't going to change your mind, are you?"

And I looked at her and said, "I really am not."

My husband was listening to all of this, and I think he knew what an asinine situation it was. He had to play along so often in his work. And even though I wouldn't this time, he never said to me, "What did you say that for?" or "You mustn't be so expressive."

That validation would help me later, long after Harry was gone.

When Mark finally told me he was gay and had AIDS, I quickly became aware of the stranglehold exerted by cultural expectations. With shame and disgust at myself, I admit that, upon receiving this terrifying news from my youngest son, my second strong reaction—the first being, *Oh, my God! My son will die!*—was *What will people think?*

I had certainly done my share of sitting quietly while jokes about "homos" were tossed out, and I knew AIDS was a sexually transmitted disease. Well, I certainly knew that "nice people" didn't get themselves into such fixes. Looked like a choice to me. How easily I sat in the seat of judgment then.

Now I was being offered a space on the hard bench of reality. It makes me think of the man who ardently opposed the death penalty—until a thief stole his car right out of his driveway. After that he altered his stance to say, "I'm against the death penalty except for car thieves." He was, of course, poking fun at himself, but the joke does bring home a point: When we are touched ourselves, the mirror defogs considerably. When the train is rushing full speed toward you, reality becomes larger than life. I knew I had to tell my close friends what was happening to my family, but I was unsure how to go about it. This was not the sort of thing one revealed at a bridge game or cocktail party—and certainly not at Sunday school. So I chose to do it in the traditional female way: at lunch.

I embarked on a series of lunches where I steered the conversation into a serious mode by prefacing my statements with, "I have something to tell you, but you have to promise not to tell anyone." My friends always promised and generally cried when they heard the awful truth, that Mark had a terminal disease that was also considered a disgrace. Not one of them condemned or criticized him.

This caring reaction comforted me, somewhat, until I realized I was telling those near and dear to me that they could not comfort one another. I had created a vow of secrecy. With that realization came the freedom to face what was ahead while I held the hands of people who loved Mark almost as much as I did.

There was the teacher who had led all of our children through four years of high school English. Later she presided over Mark's memorial service with characteristic love and humor, just as Mark would have liked.

There was his pediatrician. She had saved his life when he was three days old and experienced a life-threatening blood infection. She'd been a family friend from that time on.

There was my friend with whom I laughed and cried over all of our family growing pains, both hers and mine; the one who couldn't believe I was "pregnant again" when Mark was on the way. After all, I was 33—old enough to know better!

Of course, there were others, but not one turned from me.

Consider that I was in Asheville, a place where my husband had been highly respected as a Republican conservative, a very influential man. He was chairman of the board of directors at the Catholic Hospital, a business leader. His memory was important to me. What the community thought of us loomed large in my mind.

Harry Clarke's son is a gay man with AIDS, I imagined people saying, *and Patsy Clarke is left to deal with it. Wonder how she'll do it?*

But I valued my son more than I valued what people thought, so it didn't take me long to silence the voices in my head. I decided to tell the truth and found it to be a great thing of freedom. You don't have to watch what you're saying. What you're saying is the truth, so you're not going to trip yourself up.

Mark's death occurred right after I first moved to Raleigh. In the process of "getting on with my life," I accepted an invitation to a Woman's Club meeting. A friend thought it would be good for me to become more active. I appreciated her good intentions, so I went.

As lunch was being served, the lady on my left politely inquired, "And your name is…?"

That one was easy. I could answer that.

And then, "How many children do you have?"

I had already decided that. I could never ignore Mark's existence, so I said, "I raised four children. I have three living."

"Oh. What happened to the one who died?"

"AIDS."

It felt as if I had burped or done something equally unacceptable at the luncheon table. At the same time, it felt good to get some practice saying the difficult words, "My son died of AIDS."

I was reassured when no one gasped out loud or left the

table or said something rude. I think the poor woman who initiated the conversational gambit was taken aback, but her good manners rose to the occasion. No one had reacted in any of the ways that my society had led me to believe people would. I hope I would not have reacted that way either.

But I wasn't sure until a while later, after I had met Eloise and visited her late one afternoon.

We sat on her sunporch, where we could watch the vagabond birds taking their afternoon tea at the feeder right outside the windows. As we sipped our own tea, the conversation turned to political philosophy, as it often did with us. Eloise knew that I considered myself a conservative, and we never argued about our differing views, but we did enjoy our discussions.

On this day, Eloise leaned back in her white wicker porch rocker and said, "Let me ask you a bunch of simple questions...just for fun."

Mark Clarke's siblings, Candy, Judy, and Bruce, and his mother, Patsy, gather with him to celebrate his 31st birthday, which would be his last, at the Isle of Palms, S.C., where life had been so good to them.

I had always liked games, so I agreed.

"Do you believe in prayer in the schools?" Eloise asked.

"I've never known anyone who can keep me from praying," I responded, "and no one who can make me pray."

"What's your stand on abortion?"

"I could never have had an abortion," I said, "but I can't judge for someone else, so I guess I'm pro-choice."

"How about capital punishment?"

"I'm against it. One uncivilized act does not call for another uncivilized act. I believe in life without parole...but not execution."

"Well, I know the answer to this one," Eloise said, "but I'll put it on the list anyway: How about gay rights?"

"Of course I'm for gay rights! You know that!"

At that point, Eloise just smiled gently, and said, "Patsy, you're a liberal and don't even know it."

We sat in silence. I watched the birds leave the feeder and the sky darken. Looking at my watch, I noted the time and said I'd better get home.

Eloise told me afterward that she was afraid she had alienated me with that statement. She hadn't, but she had caused me to consider the questions she had asked and the answers I had given. My answers were not contrived, because I had replied spontaneously. They were simple, honest expressions of my beliefs.

But they suggested, perhaps, that I was not what I thought I was.

Was I was a liberal? What did that mean? Would food taste the same? Would I wear the same kinds of clothes? Would I kick over all the traces of my life in the making of new tracks?

I couldn't worry about this. I could only continue making

new tracks through many different experiences, including the friendship of many new people.

One person who stands out in my mind is Mitch Foushee. We met in June 1996, just as the MAJIC campaign was cranking up. He had been chief administrative aide to Sen. Jeff Bingamon of New Mexico and was now living in Chapel Hill and working for the Human Rights Campaign. The occasion was the coming-together of like-minded folks to work for candidates who supported human rights and, in particular, gay communities across North Carolina.

It was a hot evening in that small apartment, a portent of the scorching, humid days to come. There must have been 30 or more men and women crowded into the living-dining room area, which was separated from the tiny kitchen by only a serving bar. I had gathered some salsa and nibbles onto a wobbly paper plate and sat myself down on Mitch's very white carpet.

Never known for my grace of movement, I immediately tipped the plate over and spilled the scarlet salsa all over the white carpet. I ran into the kitchen and grabbed a wet towel and returned to the offending spot, where I scrubbed like a woman possessed. At one point I raised my eyes and met Mitch's unblinking gaze. Mortified at my awkwardness, I said, "I'm so sorry!"

He just looked at me as if to say, *Where did this person come from?*

It was not an auspicious beginning, but it actually grew into a special friendship. In fact, the whole evening brought Eloise and me many supportive friends who helped us in innumerable ways during the campaign.

Mitch and I recognized kindred souls in each other, and

he began to help MAJIC in many ways. He arranged a speaking opportunity for me in the western part of the state, and it was during this trip that he told me he had AIDS. I should have guessed, but I suppose I denied the possibility. He had so much to offer the world and did so want to give it. And he was just a little older than Mark.

Somehow I knew I would again experience the loss of someone dear to me. And I did. Mitch died less than three years later but not before he had taught me a great deal. He was such an example of intelligent compassion, something I had thought not possible in a "liberal." Looking at the political arena through his eyes helped free me to be *for* something instead of always being against an issue.

Mitch taught me that liberals could be just as upright and honest as I thought I was being when I was a conservative. I really was led to believe that liberals were scoundrels. But here was Mitch, and here was Eloise, both proving me wrong: Goodness bypasses political designations.

I remember saying one time, "It's refreshing to be a 'liberal.' Much more restful and less agitating." I also did not have to defend my position as frequently, perhaps because it made more sense.

I also had room to consider and possibly even change my mind about certain questions. Now, this is not to say that my changeover was complete. When a friend challenged me on this I reminded him that I was a "recovering Republican" and hadn't made it all the way through the 12-step program.

Today, I think I am a hybrid political animal.

In my political evolution, I occasionally encountered strong bitterness. I remember an E-mail that lashed out at me for taking so long to "come around." Defensively, I replied, "Yes, but give me credit. I have come around." This interchange came from a young gay man who probably had been so hurt for so many years that he would never forgive people like me.

Nevertheless, my newfound compatriots took my hand and dragged me down a new road. And I'm glad.

Occasionally I speak to college sociology classes on the effect of AIDS on the family, and someone always asks, "Did you lose any friends as a result of this happening in your family?"

At first the question took me aback. Even though I had been embarrassed to let people know Mark had died of AIDS, it had never occurred to me that I might lose friends because of it. Maybe that does assure me that I wouldn't have turned from someone had the roles been reversed.

My answer to the question is that if I have lost any friends, I am unaware of it. Certainly none of the people who matter to me are gone. And that was a lesson in itself. In the end, all they expressed to me was their sorrow at what was happening, and their love for Mark.

But I'm still ashamed that my second thought when I learned that Mark had AIDS was *What will people think? What will people think?*

Mostly people think about themselves, not about others. I probably ought to remember that.

Chapter Four

Eloise Vaughn: A Life in Politics

Two things I always did with great energy: raise children and campaign.

My belly huge and round, my dress flat against me in the summer heat, I would drive every county road if I had to, in order to get my husband, Earl, elected to county, then state office.

Once, I was so determined to get every country store owner to post one of Earl's campaign signs in his window that I drove into another state without knowing it.

"I'd hang the sign, ma'am," the grocer told me, "but you're in Virginia."

It was all worth it, because Earl Vaughn made it all the way from country lawyer to the North Carolina Supreme Court. He even had his picture taken with John F. Kennedy, back when the future president was a young senator. I have the photo in the den of our house in Raleigh.

Of course I'm still there; North Carolina is all I know.

I was born in Chapel Hill in 1932, the middle of three children. My older brother, Avery, was 10 years older, and my other brother, John, is two years younger. My mother was raised by her father and a stepmother. But her father was very strict, and you weren't supposed to do anything on Sunday except go to church and contemplate.

One Sunday afternoon my mother went down to the creek to watch some friends who were fishing. Someone told her father, and when she got home she got the worst whipping she had ever gotten for defiling the Sabbath.

So when we were young, we weren't supposed to do anything on the Lord's day. We couldn't play cards or dance in the house. Mother thought it was terrible when people rode up and down the street in their cars or went shopping on Sundays. She was just aghast. We weren't supposed to go to movies on Sunday, although I do think we slipped up when we were in high school. She didn't hold us to those strict standards when we got older, but she still didn't approve.

That's how strict a background I came from. But it has helped me all my life.

We spent Saturdays getting ready for church on Sunday, cleaning up the house and the yard and ourselves. Mother did a lot of the cooking for Sundays. And then every week, the Orange United Methodist Church was full of our kin and neighbors.

My family was an old-fashioned, extended Southern family. Family reunions occurred often at our house because we lived in what was called "the home place." Dozens of aunts, uncles, and cousins visited us all the time, especially on Sunday afternoons. We got together to make ice cream on summer afternoons and to enjoy Sunday dinners throughout the year.

They'd all sit on the porch, and recall everything about everyone. Things like, "Old Uncle So-and-So went off to Macon, Georgia, and never came back. He had five daughters, and he heard that Macon was an up-and-coming place to find husbands for them all."

Or they'd talk about how their father—my grandfather—had suffered in the Civil War, how he came home with what today would probably be called post-traumatic stress disorder.

My own father had returned from serving in France during World War I, his health permanently impaired. He came to live with his elderly, widowed mother on the home place and tried to farm those rocky fields. He married my mother, who lived with them on 120 rolling acres covered with large areas of trees, huge boulders, open fields and pastures, and two meandering creeks.

In 1929, after the death of my grandmother, the house and all its contents burned to the ground. Somehow, with a loan from the bank, Mother and Daddy built a new and somewhat larger house. But then the Depression spread its hardships all over this country. Just making those bank payments became an overwhelming specter. But they were made, and except for the sale of a small parcel of land "on the backside," the farm remained ours.

My father was influenced by his oldest brother, Charles Maddry, who was the executive director of the Southern Baptist Convention. He was liberal, and so was the SBC at that time. My uncle was a missionary who traveled all over the world but always came back to the home place to be renewed. Still, he was very large in his outlook.

Uncle Charles worked his way through the University of North Carolina in the early 1900s and became a Baptist

Mark Vaughn with his father, Earl, and mother, Eloise, in 1973 at the Farm House, where he performed for two summers.

minister before heading the SBC, which he saved from bankruptcy during the Depression. A scholar and writer, he had a bright, inquiring mind and was as beloved by his black brothers and he was by his white ones.

Uncle Charles had an abiding love for his alma mater, UNC, and for its president, Frank Porter Graham, who later ran in an infamous North Carolina Senate campaign against Willis Smith. During the race there was a great deal of negative advertising, which we had never seen in North Carolina before. It's worth noting that Jesse Helms first cut his political teeth as an adviser to Smith.

My family was a very proud family, but they were not pretentious. In fact, they derided pretentiousness, and I think that had a lot to do with my later fight against hypocrisy in the church and society in general.

My beliefs were also shaped by my teachers in the

Chapel Hill schools. Attending these schools during the Depression and the war years gave me an immeasurable advantage. Because Chapel Hill is a university town, we had the best teachers anywhere.

From there, I went on to the University of North Carolina, Chapel Hill, where I was able to sit in classes taught by some of the greatest teachers that institution has ever known. This experience opened my world and guided my intellect.

It was at UNC where I met Earl Vaughn.

Earl had been to Korea, and had come back to law school at UNC on the GI Bill. He was raised on a tobacco farm in Rockingham County. The things I admired most about Earl were his mind and his great sense of humor. Everything else followed.

We wanted to get married, and Earl wanted to go back to his home county to practice law, so he told me to hurry up my education. I went year-round and completed my college degree in 2½ years. I had to maintain at least a B average because otherwise they wouldn't let me finish early. What I did for love! We were married on December 20, 1952, the day after I finished my final exams. I was 20 years old.

But I was to receive an entirely new kind of education as I helped my husband participate in the democratic process of the county—and state—where we lived.

Earl started out as a young lawyer in a small mill-centered town, so we didn't enjoy the large income associated with lawyers. But we were making so many new friends and enjoying our life together. We felt free and independent and, despite what may have seemed a small income, self-sufficient and comfortable.

Then came the day Earl was elected to the state general assembly. What an unbelievable victory that was: a small-town, country lawyer facing down another young attorney from an old, well-respected family.

But Earl wanted to participate in the governing process. This had been one of his lifelong interests and, finally, a personal goal. And he did it almost alone. I remember paying high school girls 50 cents an hour to help me fold, stuff, and seal thousands of letters to send to constituents in our county. His first successful race was for the office of prosecuting attorney. How sweet it was to win, especially when, as they say in the South, no one would have bet a plugged nickel on us.

We had Mark in 1955. Three years later, in 1958, we had another son, John, a hard worker who has always tried to please us. I saw his wife's engagement ring even before she did, and I even tried it on because he wanted me to see it first. That's how much he wanted approval and to know that what he was doing was right. He and his wife, Cheri, lead busy, happy lives and have two wonderful girls.

Stuart Earl, born in 1960, is my freckled-faced, red-curled boy. He was born the year his father was first elected to the state legislature. Even though Earl was away a lot, as a child "His Stuart" was always diligent and never a worry. When he was in college, he painted houses in the summer and worked during winter cutting down Christmas trees. Today, he sells electrical equipment and is the father of two boys with his wife, Shay.

And then there's Rose, the baby and our only girl, born in 1964. She's always had great expectations for herself. In high school she was on the student council and later was president of her class. She graduated from UNC-Chapel

Hill and then earned a degree from its law school. She is now a partner in a law firm. Rose is very close to me, and she's the only person I know who'll tell me, "Don't buy that sweater. It looks terrible on you." That's how close we are; she speaks to me like a friend.

Rose and her husband, Jon, have one son, and in March 2000 she gave birth to a little girl, Eloise Rose. I was so touched by the gesture of having the baby named after me that for the longest time I didn't know what to call her. I didn't feel worthy of having this beautiful baby named for me.

When Mark died, I called Rose right away, and she and Jon began the hour-long drive from Goldsboro to Raleigh to be with me. Partly to soothe themselves, they had their car radio tuned to National Public Radio. The news that day included a broadcast of a speech Jesse Helms was making on the floor of the U.S. Senate. As Rose and Jon listened, Helms raved at length in opposition to the re-funding of the Ryan White Bill, which provides federal money for places hardest hit by AIDS. It helps those with no resources of their own to get medicine and treatment.

Helms's tone was self-righteous, acidic, and hurtful to gay people and their families. What he essentially said was that those who died of AIDS or who were living with AIDS deserved it because they had "brought it upon themselves."

Rose and Jon were horrified, and because it was coming at them at this most desolate time, Rose broke down immediately.

She later said, "I wanted to tell Senator Helms that I wondered if he could, at that moment, take my mother's hands in his, look her in the eyes, and say the same things about her son, my beloved brother, now deceased for two hours."

As my own children grew, so did my political knowledge.

Those early days were an exciting time. In North Carolina, the wives of members of the general assembly, council of state, and judges, along with those in the university system, formed a quasisocial group called the Sir Walter Cabinet (named for Sir Walter Raleigh, for whom our capital city is named). In the 1950s and '60s, when I arrived, proper attire was de rigueur. It would be unheard of to appear at a meeting without hat and gloves.

So, with skills I'd learned years earlier, I sewed my own dresses, suits, coats, and even hats. It took a lot of self-confidence and courage for me to go down to Raleigh so attired. But I loved every minute of it and was proud to stand by with all four children when, seven years after he first went to Raleigh, Earl was elected speaker of the house. Later we stood as he was sworn onto the Court of Appeals and, after that, the Supreme Court.

I taught junior high school for 15 years and worked as a receptionist at the North Carolina state legislature for six years, learning the names and the way things worked. I watched my husband and soaked in everything, especially the lessons of some of North Carolina's great leaders and thinkers: Luther Hodges, Terry Sanford, and Gov. Jim Hunt. I watched and listened and learned. I always agreed with and fully supported Earl's involvement with the Democratic Party and the causes and positions for which he fought. I loved to be with him as much as I could as he progressed, but more than anything, I stayed active with the county Democratic Women. I have been a member of the Democratic Women of Rockingham County, and now Wake County, for 45 years; have spent 18 years with the Woman's Club; and, for more than 30 years, have been a member of the Edenton Street United Methodist Church in Raleigh.

All of these associations and all of that knowledge would give me the grounding I would need later in life.

Just months after he took a seat on the North Carolina Supreme Court in 1985, Earl was diagnosed with lung cancer, which had metastasized to his brain. He had finally reached the pinnacle of his career only to learn that his life was about to end.

And there I was beside him, as I was at the start, holding his hand, trying to boost his spirits, and then, later, soothing my family. I never let anyone forget what a good man, an honest and true man, he had been. He was 56 years old when he died.

Years later I carried out the same duties for Mark. I helplessly watched him negotiate the start of his adult life, I cared for him, and then I comforted him until the end.

I was like my mother in that way; of all the people to guide me in my life—church leaders, teachers, and political leaders—she had the greatest influence on me. She was a patient, giving person, ever self-sacrificing for all of us, including her grandchildren. She was a great example of determination, moral strength, compassion, and undying devotion to her family and friends.

Mark told me one day, when he was quite ill, that he wanted to go see his daddy and his grandma. My mother had died when she was 86, still in her Sunday clothes and pearls. She had always been so morally strong that Mark knew that if there was a heaven, Grandma had to be there.

I told him to go. And I think this made it easier for him to die.

When he did, I started to campaign, as I had for Earl all those years before. And instead of a seat in state government, it was for compassion and understanding.

When we founded MAJIC, I learned quickly that the script had changed and I was in the rough arena. The fact that I knew how to get things done politically was a help. Only now I was the speaker, saying to everyone I had known in my life, "Help me fight for what I know to be right. It's not right for anyone to target a minority who has never had a voice to speak for themselves."

I had no idea whether we could keep Jesse Helms from winning another term in the U.S. Senate in 1996. I did believe, though, that we had a niche to fill. We could be a little drop feeding into the big stream of the Democratic Party. We could energize those already fighting in the contest for the Senate. I even thought that because we were a different little stream, we could attract those who would otherwise never have anything to do with politics or a Senate race.

I knew that if anything was going to be accomplished, I had to believe in its goodness, necessity, and rightness. I had to be willing to lay everything on the line to bring it to pass. I had to be prepared to risk everything I was, or had, to accomplish it. I had to work, engaging my heart, my soul, and all my energy. I had to focus my entire life on that goal.

I learned this from the earliest days of my life. I learned that, though others may sympathize and sometimes offer help, when it comes right down to it, you have to do things yourself. You must fight your own battles. No one else is going to do that for you.

It was that way with helping my family, as a child. It was that way when I went to school and graduated early to marry Earl. It was that way when Earl ran for office, when I raised my children to be good and strong. It was that way when Earl was no longer strong and that way years later when Mark told me he was gay and had AIDS. It was that way when he died.

Each time, I assessed a situation's goodness, necessity, and rightness, then risked everything to accomplish it. And never have I been disappointed, only proud. Through these challenges, I found my own independence, and through all these people, I had become my own person.

Chapter Five

MOTHERS UNITED THROUGH THEIR MARKS

Eloise has said that our first meeting was almost like an accident.

"There aren't any accidents," I always tell her. "You know that."

Mark Clarke had been dead for just a few weeks. I was in the mall with my son Bruce, who was trying to get me out and help me start to "get better." I'd lost my son, and my husband had died a few years before, and I think you could call me bereft. I sure was going under. So what do you do? You go out and get a change of scenery and hear living noises and be where people are.

We bumped into a colleague of Bruce's and his wife, who knew about Mark's death.

"How're you doing?" the wife asked me.

"Oh, well, you know..." I didn't know.

"I know a woman just like you," she said. "A woman who's also lost a son to AIDS. And she does great things and goes around and talks about it and tries to help other people. I'm going to go home and call her and tell her to call you."

"Oh, thanks...yes, well..." I was casual, detached. Everything felt like a cliché.

I paid no attention to this woman or what she was saying. The weight of my grief made it impossible to raise my head, or my consciousness, to anything.

I had barely gotten in the door that evening when the phone rang.

"Is this Patsy Clarke?" a woman's voice asked when I answered. It was a warm Southern voice.

"Yes," I sighed, when I really wanted to say, "No, and I don't want any aluminum siding."

"My name is Eloise Vaughn. I understand you've lost a son to AIDS," the voice said. "So have I."

For so long, I had felt like I was wading through a morass of misery—and hadn't met anyone who could show me a bridge to the other side. Until now. This woman would understand what I was thinking and how I was feeling.

We agreed to meet for lunch. I learned later that this is one of the things Eloise does. Whenever she hears of a woman who has lost a son to AIDS, she extends her heart and her hand.

Months later I asked Eloise who she expected to meet that day...a weeping, wailing mother? She had no idea, she told me. She had met so many women who had lost sons in the four years since her Mark had died. She didn't expect anything but for us to talk with an eagerness and empathy that comes when you meet another person who has had to bury a child. A beautiful son. Named Mark.

Eloise never expected this meeting to develop into a friendship. Most of the women she has met have been very

70

nice and then returned to their own church circles, committee meetings, cancer drives, whatever. The association would always end.

But this would be different.

We met for lunch at Simpson's, a steak house in a shopping center not far from our respective homes.

My first impression of Eloise was that she was pretty and well put together. I could easily see her entertaining important guests at a reception, as she looked like the classic hostess. She knew how to put people at ease, and she did that with me. Eloise was immediately kind and generous of spirit. She seemed to genuinely care about my very recent and raw loss. I felt that she, more than anyone else, understood. She had walked on the same path.

We sipped tea and showed pictures of our Marks, connecting the way women do. As we shared our stories and talked about our sons, we realized there was a commonality in thinking, an interest we couldn't ignore—and so many coincidences.

Both of our sons were named Mark—and that seemed huge to us. Both were in the entertainment industry: theater and television. Both of us had led very mainstream, privileged lives. Our husbands were both politically involved, but they were in different parties. We both had four children. Each of us was widowed before our sons died, so each of us had to deal with that trauma alone. Neither of us had known that our sons were gay, although both of us had had suspicions about their sexuality.

At the end of the meal, the waiter asked if we would like dessert.

"I'd like a glass of wine," I said. I'd hesitated at the start of the meal, not wanting her to think I was some sort of lush.

"Oh, so would I," Eloise said. She told me she had held back from wine too, afraid of what I would think. It seemed ridiculous to have worried about that now, with all we had laid out between us. The wine came, and we stayed and talked for another hour or so.

When I left, I felt a sense of catharsis. Eloise was able to listen to me and I to her, and, unlike with family members, we felt like we weren't hurting each other in speaking our minds. We weren't afraid to talk about the one who was gone—without causing tears. We were able to say what needed to be said about how much we missed our sons, how much we loved them. And we were able to ask out loud: How did this happen, and what could we have done to keep this from happening? Nothing, we assured each other. There was nothing we could have done.

At another lunch we found that both our Marks were irresponsible with money and that each had owned a linen suit—Mark Clarke's in white, Mark Vaughn's in pink.

"Can you imagine if they had met?" I asked. "We could have been mothers-in-law."

Even though our friendship had a solid base, it still moved step by step.

Neither of us wanted to be living in each other's pocket and have lunch every Tuesday. We would see each other when we had something to tell each other, and we kept up on a pretty regular basis. Maybe Eloise would call every six weeks, or I'd call and say I'm going away, but let's have lunch when I get back.

We grew close gradually, but every time we'd meet, we'd find we had a waterfall of things to say. Our lunchtime had run out, we had eaten all our food, finished our wine, and we'd still be bubbling over and talking.

Patsy and Eloise at a MAJIC meeting in November 1999.

There was also so much for us to learn from each other.

Eloise taught me to be more patient. She taught me to be gentler. But then, she also helped me to get tough. Eloise was the one to convince me that Jesse Helms was not a friend—and it took a bit of work.

One day while we pored over plates of slippery linguine, Eloise pulled a newspaper clipping out of her purse.

"Well, my conservative buddy," she began, "have you seen the editorial in *The Raleigh News & Observer*?"

"No...what?"

"Jesse Helms said that people who die of AIDS deserve what they got."

Eloise was hitting me where it hurt. She knew it too. She didn't want to cause me pain, but she did want me to see what was going on in the world that I was ignoring.

"Are you sure?" I asked.

"Absolutely. I clipped it, and here it is."

She handed me a copy of the newspaper dated June 2, 1995. The editorial read, in part:

> The senator implies that because HIV is spread through risky behavior, AIDS sufferers deserve their fate.... But to suggest that AIDS victims have it coming and should be punished with medical neglect is no more acceptable than to begrudge a heart bypass for, say, a 70-year-old senator who spent years smoking tobacco and eating barbecue.

I can still recall the disbelief I felt, how I thought there must have been a mistake.

But Eloise sat there knowingly, and so did later stories from the newspaper, dated July 1995, chronicling Helms's fight to restrict the Ryan White Care Act.

> WASHINGTON—Sen. Jesse Helms, in a biting speech aimed at "the homosexual lobby," vowed Friday to fight a bill that funds medical treatment for AIDS victims.
>
> During debate on the Senate floor, Helms reaffirmed controversial comments he made about homosexuality last month.
>
> "Sure, I said it was a filthy, disgusting practice," Helms said. "I said it, I meant it, and I repeat it today."

In another story, dated July 27, Helms said: "I hate to use the word 'gay' in connection with sodomy. There is nothing gay about these people. 'Gay' used to be a beautiful word, but it has been corrupted by these people."

I went home and thought about all of this. I thought about my daughter, Judy, saying so many times, "Mom, you ought to write to Senator Helms about Mark. You ought to stand up for your son and others like him, and for AIDS research. You could make a difference because Senator Helms knew Dad. Dad was his friend. I don't see how you cannot write to him."

I didn't know how I could write to a powerful senator. What would a man like Jesse Helms care what I thought? So I'd resisted Judy's urgings, because I feared I would fail. And I don't like to fail, or to have my illusions destroyed.

But after that lunch with Eloise, I went home and wrote the letter on yellow legal paper. And I cried as I did it, thinking, *Who do I think I am?*

I am Mark's mother, I told myself. *And I will stand up for him.*

June 5, 1995
Senator Jesse Helms
U.S. Senate
Washington, D.C.

Dear Jesse,

When my husband (and your strong friend) Harry Clarke died in a plane crash at the Asheville airport on March 9, 1987, you called me in the night. You told me of your sorrow at our loss and of what Harry had meant to you as a friend. You placed your praise for him and his principles in the Congressional Record. You sent me the flag flown over the capitol in his memory. You did all of these things and I am grateful.

Harry and I had a son, Mark, who was almost the image of his father, though much taller. He was blessed with great charm and intelligence, and we loved him. He was gay. On March 9, 1994, exactly seven years to the day that his father died, Mark followed him—a victim of AIDS. I sat by his bed, held his dear hand and sang through that long, last night the baby song that I had sung to all our children: "Rock-a-bye and don't you cry, rock-a-bye little Mark. I'll buy you a pretty gold horse to ride all around your pasture..."

A few days before he died, Mark said these words: "This disease is not beating me. When I draw my last breath I will have defeated this disease—and I will be free." I watched him take his last breath and claim his freedom. He was 31.

As I write these words, I relive the most difficult time of my life. The tears will smudge this if I don't take care. No matter, I will type it so it is legible. My reason for writing to you is not to plead for funds, although I'd like to ask your support for AIDS research; it is not to accept a lifestyle which is abhorrent to you; it is rather to ask you not to pass judgment on other human beings as "deserving what they get." No one deserves that. AIDS is not a disgrace, it is a TRAGEDY. Nor is homosexuality a disgrace; we so-called normal people make it a tragedy because of our own lack of understanding.

Mark gave me a great gift. A quote returns to me from long-ago forensic days: "I have no lamp to light my feet save the lamp of experience." I think Patrick Henry said it. Mark's life and death have illuminated my own, and I am grateful for him.

So, that's what this letter is about, and I hope I have written it well. I wish you had known Mark. His life was so much more eloquent than any words I might put on paper. I ask you to share his memory with me in compassion.

Gratefully,
Patsy M. Clarke

I felt a sense of relief. I had done the best I knew how. I had not asked for too much—just compassion. And I had not turned my back on my son's memory.

Two weeks later the answer came, and I tore the letter open. Surely Jesse was the man I believed him to be. He was going to say he understood, that he was sorry.

I couldn't have been more wrong.

June 19, 1995

Dear Patsy,

I hope you will forgive my first-naming you. Having known Harry as I did and having read your poignant letter, I just don't feel like being formal in this response.

I know that Mark's death was devastating to you. As for homosexuality, the Bible judges it, I do not. I do take the position that there must be some reasonableness in allocation of federal funds for research, treatment, etc. There is no justification for AIDS funding far exceeding that for other killer diseases such as cancer, heart trouble, etc.

And, by the way, the news media have engaged in their usual careless selves by reporting that I am "holding up" the authorizing legislation that includes AIDS funding. One of the homosexual activists sent out a totally erroneous press release (and he knew what he was saying was not true) hoping to cause me problems. He failed. I did file a "notify" request because I have two or three amendments that I intend to offer to restore balance to the spending of the taxpayers' money for research and treatment of various diseases.

I understand the militant homosexuals and they understand me. They climbed onto the roof of Dot's and my home and hoisted a giant canvas condom.

As for Mark, I wish he had not played Russian roulette in his sexual activity. He obviously had a very great deal to offer to the uplifting of his generation. He did not live to do all of the wonderful things that he might otherwise have done.

I have sympathy for him—and for you. But there is no escaping the reality of what happened.

I wish you well always.

Sincerely,
Jesse H.

I cried. I walked the floor. I agonized for two or three days, and then I got mad.

What made me the angriest was that Jesse didn't understand what I'd written. All he talked about in that letter was the fact that "the militant homosexuals…had hoisted a giant canvas condom" on his house.

I had nothing to do with that. My letter had nothing to do with that. He missed the point entirely. The greatest thing that could have happened would have been for Jesse to be like Paul on the road to Damascus, and have one of those "Ah-ha!" moments. He doesn't realize how he has made so many people suffer.

The only thing that would have made me feel better is if Jesse had retracted his statement about AIDS patients deserving what they get, if he'd stated that he really didn't mean it that way. But he never even referred to that statement in the letter. He never denied it or acknowledged it. He ignored it.

He was trying to get his point across, Eloise said, that homosexuals deserve to die, and that this AIDS business is too bad, but homosexuals bring it on themselves. We wonder why Jesse Helms hates homosexuals. What is it he is doing? Taking refuge in meanness? In sanctimoniousness?

Megan, Alan, and Erin Clarke made this banner for their Uncle Mark. Their father, Bruce, took it to Mark during his last days in West Palm Beach, Fla. It hung on the wall where Mark could see it.

In self-righteousness? Does he find safety there?

Eloise believes that what Helms says strikes a chord with people because it reaches to their own prejudices, and that makes them say "Yeah! That's the way I feel too. Jesse says what I feel." She says this is what the senator has done with anyone not as conservative as he. This time, his target was gay people.

But really his attitude stems from fear. Such dislike—it even approaches hatred—is irrational. I know from my own experience that examination of long-held beliefs can be frightening. What if what I've long accepted as "the way it is" turns out to be wrong?

Truth can shed a harsh light on a subject. Again I am reminded of Paul on the road to Damascus, where he lost his sight in order to gain it. A painful process—much like being set adrift without a compass or an oar. But the winds of truth can push you ashore. Eloise and I certainly discovered that. Eloise never had to deny that her son was gay, but I did. I think I denied. I know I denied. But then I think: I just hid it briefly.

In the months following the letter exchange, a lot of things happened.

One of the best was that the Senate approved the Ryan White CARE Act, which paid for AIDS research and treated AIDS patients. It passed 97–3—Jesse, joined by senators Jon Kyl of Arizona and Robert C. Smith of New Hampshire, opposed the bill.

"There is a great odor rising from the manner in which Congress is falling all over itself to do what the homosexual lobby is almost hysterically demanding," Helms said on the Senate floor.

He had proposed three amendments to the bill. One would have frozen federal spending on AIDS research and treatment for five years, and the second would have limited spending to the amounts laid out for cancer research and treatment.

Helms said the government spends $2.7 billion a year on AIDS, compared to $2.3 billion on cancer. Sen. Nancy Kassenbaum countered Helms by saying that his figures did not include the bulk of cancer funds associated with mandatory programs such as Medicare and Medicaid. Those programs, she said, boosted total federal spending to $34 billion for heart disease, $15 billion for cancer, and $5.4 billion for AIDS.

Despite his defeat, Helms felt good—good enough to announce that he would seek his fifth six-year term in the Senate. (He was challenged by Charlotte mayor Harvey Gantt.) Jesse had been swept into the Senate in 1972, after serving as the city editor of *The Raleigh Times* and, in 1960, becoming a commentator for WRAL-TV in Raleigh.

Eloise and I stewed about what to do about what had, until now, been a private battle between Jesse Helms and myself. What positive and constructive action could we take in memory of our sons?

We talked about getting the other mothers of AIDS victims together to talk about this injustice and other issues, but the plan seemed to go completely against us. We tried to get a meeting announcement in the AIDS Service Agency bulletin, but it didn't go in for one reason or another. It certainly was not anyone's desire to keep us from doing it, but the ASA said it couldn't sponsor a mothers' meeting and wouldn't give us any names for privacy reasons.

So we found the names ourselves. Eloise knew everyone. She was a former ASA volunteer and board member, and had lived in Raleigh for years, so she knew a lot of people. She was the leader in that sense, and got MAJIC going.

By contrast, the people I've always known would not have even discussed AIDS. We would have swept it under the rug. But I didn't have to do that with this new friend. And that was different. So much was different with Eloise. There was never a time when I said to myself, *This is going to be a really solid, longtime friend.* I have had those moments with people, and generally I've been wrong.

This friendship, with Eloise, crept up on me. And it has been as varied and unexpected as the weather.

We had a strong beginning: We both had loved our sons, and we both had lost them. It was the first knot in the rope of friendship. We came to learn that we both believe in the strength of our love for our families. We both laugh a lot—often at each other, but also to offset the teasing of others.

Eloise and I have been accused of being a "traveling road show," and I guess there is a sense of the comedic about us. We are, after all, two grandmothers clutching their purses, who ventured into a very dissonant world, part of which did everything to discourage our involvement. We both talk too much, at high speed, at high volume, at the same time, and we still never miss a syllable of each other's side of the conversation.

There are days when we don't always see eye to eye on things: Eloise still has hope that the church can be what it claims to be. I am more pessimistic about human nature. She has great faith in the political process, especially the Democratic Party. Again, I am the pessimist.

But our similarities are much greater than our differences. We became even stronger after many experiences together—some hysterical, some heartbreaking. We were tested with disagreements. But we would find that the rope of our friendship was strong enough to withstand the strongest pulls.

I know there will always be an Eloise. I think she knows there will always be a Patsy. And just as it was at that first lunch, we'll always have our Marks with us.

Chapter Six

WHY WE HAD TO ACT

We didn't want a grief group.

There are a lot of grief groups around, and they serve a wonderful purpose. We didn't feel the need for that; we were handling our grief. What we needed was some way to take action—and we needed others like us to move us along.

We needed a mothers' group.

Eloise got a list of mothers who happened to be about our age because, of course, that's usually when you lose your son to AIDS. In fact, we later learned that in the U.S. one third of the people with AIDS were dependent on a parent for financial, physical, and emotional support. For several years the American Association of Retired Persons has been trying to enlighten older adults about the ways their lives can be affected by AIDS—and to find ways to help them.

Eloise and I were also trying to find a way to take action while at the same time helping ourselves and standing up for our sons. Jesse Helms—with his impassioned, antigay rhetoric and shameless fight against funding AIDS research—was our biggest obstacle. He was also the enemy in our own backyard. And he was seeking his fifth six-year term in the Senate later that year.

As Eloise and I saw it, our mission was clear.

So we called our mothers' group together. In absolute honesty, Eloise and I had had something like this in mind for a long time, but we were afraid to call the mothers together and say, "Well, fellas, we're gonna start a political action committee, and we're gonna go out and get Jesse Helms." We figured we might scare them all away. We were a little scared about it ourselves. What were we thinking?

Eloise and I would have both backed away if we hadn't had each other to keep feeding on.

The first time all the mothers met—about 10 of us in my living room—we didn't say a thing about starting a formal campaign. Instead, we let every mother tell the story of her son, and someone walking in would have probably thought it was a grief group. But it wasn't. It was an explanation. It was saying, *This was my son. I loved him. I love him now. This is what I experienced.* We went around the room, and it was cathartic, so in that sense it related to grief. It took most of an afternoon, and we had tea and coffee and went through a few boxes of tissues.

When we finished, Eloise and I introduced our plan: "We were just thinking...of course, this sounds so funny...that maybe...because of this thing that Jesse said...isn't this awful?...how does that make you feel?"

And they were just as animated as mother bears protecting their cubs—sitting up, moving around in their seats, suddenly anxious: "He said that? Oh, that old...!" I won't

86

tell you what they called him, because it isn't nice for mothers to talk like that.

I ventured ahead. "We were thinking of getting together and trying to fight Jesse's attitude," I said. "My daughter, Candy, suggested we call it Mothers Against Jesse in Congress. We could call ourselves MAJIC." Well, there was so much laughter, and then everyone looked at each other and said, "What a good idea."

At the second meeting, we firmed up their support for taking political action. When several of the mothers offered checks for $25, we were nonplussed. What to do with them?

First off, I went into my kitchen and got a clean pickle jar, which became our first bank. As the meeting broke up, I stood at the front door saying, "Thank you for coming." The last guest to leave my entry hall was the tiniest mother present. I myself am not very tall, but I towered over Stephanie, a little dove of a woman who was wearing a pretty print dress. She paused at the door, looked up at me, and her eyes misted over. "Kevin would be so proud."

Her Kevin had died a difficult death, and I know she felt unable to help him. But now, in a way, she could.

My idea—this is how silly I was—was to have some little cards printed that said "MAJIC" and, underneath, "Mothers Against Jesse in Congress." Wouldn't say anything more. We would go to restaurants and we would leave a little card when we had lunch, or we'd go into the restroom and wash our hands and leave a little card. I had no notion that we were going to end up in *People* magazine or in the political pages of *The New York Times* or as number 3 on Jesse Helms's political enemies list. I never thought that far. If I'd known, I probably would have turned tail and run.

A group of MAJIC members and their supporters outside the Smithsonian Institute during a visit to the Names Quilt exhibition in Washington, D.C., in October 1996. The mothers displayed their handsewn banner at all their rallies.

We were just going to stand up and say, "Hey, we're a bunch of mothers who think our sons were good people, and we're sorry that someone like our senator would think they deserved what they got." That's all we had in mind. And we got swept along as if by a tidal wave. Our heads were above water, but our bodies were just paddling as hard as we could to keep going.

It seemed fitting that our printer was called Grass Roots Printing, even though we often felt more like weeds than grass. We had a burning passion, and that was about all. We had no notion of what a political campaign meant. Or at least, I didn't. Eloise had always been involved in politics through her husband, but she had never been on the firing line herself.

So here we went, into the human morass that is filled with monumental egos and much more. In the beginning,

MAJIC was just Eloise and me with the mothers as the cheering section in the background. Very quickly, we realized MAJIC was bigger than that.

At one meeting we attended to gauge our support, we met some women who had already established a political action committee called North Carolina Cares. After a brief discussion with them we realized they knew a whole lot more than we did (that wasn't difficult) and arranged to meet with them. We were worse than novices in the political action world, and this group seemed savvy.

We met at a local cafeteria and, over meat loaf and Jell-O, forged a partnership we thought would spare us of all the organizational ills that frightened us. We would go about the land speaking our message and raising money in our efforts to defeat the sitting senator, and North Carolina Cares would file all the forms and handle the finances. A pipe dream!

I am now reminded of another old saw: "If it sounds too good to be true, it probably is."

Very shortly after our happy agreement with this already established PAC, we were scheduled to make an appearance at a Democratic Women's Club meeting. At the end of the luncheon, complete with remarks castigating Republicans (the rhetoric is the same on both sides, I discovered…only the labels differ), we pointed to a large fishbowl and asked for donations for our efforts, which totaled about $32. We thought this was wonderful. Just think! People believed in what we were doing and were willing to donate money to our cause!

Flushed with success, we rushed over to the NC Cares office (they even had an office) and dutifully turned over our $32 to the person in charge. If you ever need an image of two naïve old ladies, we were it.

Very quickly we realized we were not going to be compatible with NC Cares. While some of the aims were certainly similar, the means by which we wanted to accomplish them differed greatly. Without belaboring all of the circumstances (catfights are never very fascinating), let's just say we came to a parting of ways. It wasn't quite the Red Sea, but big enough for us.

I received a call one morning saying in cultured and courteous tones that "it will be better if MAJIC goes its own way, separate from NC Cares, effective immediately." Realizing that our first batch of brochures went to the printer that day and would carry the logo of NC Cares, I all but begged the courteous voice to reconsider and at least give us a bit of time.

"No-o-o," she said patiently, and suggested we apply for nonprofit status or some such thing. I asked for our records and a check for whatever little bit we had accumulated. She instructed me to go to the home of their treasurer and that all of our material would await us.

Well, before I could do that, something had to be done about the brochures, which at that moment were heading into the printing press. I called our wonderful printer and said something akin to "Stop the presses!" and that we had to regroup. He couldn't have been nicer, and he gave a great low laugh as he said, "I guess sometimes our running late is a good thing. Don't worry. Just call when you're ready."

And, of course, we did.

Eloise and I knew we had to do something about our status. We couldn't remain just two rebel grandmothers with a cause. Whereas we had started out as mama bears protecting our cubs who had been attacked, we weren't attempting to play in the real and frightening world of "big boy politics."

The Federal Election Commission couldn't care less that we had "noble intentions." What mattered to them was that the forms were filled out correctly and that the filings were on time. We didn't even have the forms, much less know how to fill them out.

Another old saying fits here: "God takes care of fools and old women."

We knew a lawyer who qualified as both friend and legal adviser. Coincidentally, he was the last person to see my husband alive, as he had taken Harry to the airstrip that awful night the plane went down. He was also a friend of some 40 years to Eloise and her family. Another good sign. We both trusted him and felt safe with his advice.

There we sat on Eloise's sunporch, asking him where to sign and deciding who would be the chairman of the PAC and who would be the secretary-treasurer. The instructions were daunting, to say the least. This was the first (of what proved to be many more) times that I wished I could get out of this fix I was in.

We didn't really know what we were doing. We were just driven by almost primal emotions. So we signed where he told us to, and we mailed it in just under the deadline for the filing requirement. When we realized we would have to make quarterly reports, we took Scarlett O'Hara's route: We would think about that tomorrow.

Just before we finished our instructional meeting with our lawyer friend, I looked at him and said, "Sam, what would Harry think about what I'm doing?"

You see, I still worried over my defection from the ranks of conservatism and Jesse's supporters. But it's hard to change your course when you're close to the destination. Sam looked at me with a face that gave nothing away and said, "I think he'd be glad that you're involved with the process."

Fairly noncommittal, I know. But I was beginning to understand that I could not keep seeking approval for actions I had to take.

Our own "coming out" as a political action committee was a rally that we called "A Gathering of Mothers," held on the grounds of the state capitol in Raleigh on May 11, 1996, the day before Mother's Day. An appropriate time for a circle of mothers to launch an audacious project.

"MAJIC moments for Mother's Day in May," our brochure read. "Take a moment, take a stand. Have a voice as well as a vote in your choice of who represents you and your family in our society. Hate, prejudice, and bigotry are not family values! Regardless of your status, culture, race, or creed...if you are a mother (or have one) it matters."

Eloise and I had made a giant Mother's Day card out of two, 8-foot-by-4-foot styrofoam panels that we bordered with wallpaper printed with words such as LOVE, PEACE, HOPE, and JOY. The message read: MOTHER'S DAY GREETINGS, SENATOR HELMS, FROM THE FAMILIES OF NORTH CAROLINA. OUR WISH: A LAND WITHOUT BIGOTRY, JUDGMENTALISM, HATRED. A LAND WITH COMPASSION, UNDERSTANDING, LOVE.

We planned to have people sign it at the rally, then deliver it to Jesse's office in Raleigh or Washington, D.C., soon after. The giant card would later become one of our trademarks.

The morning of the rally reminded me of the children's book *Ferdinand the Bull* by Munro Leaf, wherein he describes the bull ring: "What a day it was! Flags were flying and all the lovely ladies had flowers in their hair!"

We didn't have flowers in our hair, but we sure had flowers all over our dresses. I remember how carefully I'd picked out my attire for that day. I had no experience selecting what a mother turned political activist would wear. My long skirt had colorful flowers printed all over it, and I chose a plain white blouse to go with it. I think, in my case, hysteria was the motif of the day. I kept thinking, *What am I doing here? I should be home under the bed where I belong, where no one will laugh or point fingers at me.*

The wind was blowing everything that wasn't nailed down that day, but we felt grounded and secure as the crowd started to grow. There was music, laughter, and lots of talking with wonder about what was happening around us.

The atmosphere was that of a circus, with people of all ages, card tables filled with strange and interesting items standing unevenly on the grass. We had fans like those commonly used at old-time Southern funeral services, which bore Jesse's face, replete with a cross mark across it. There were MAJIC buttons and bumper stickers featuring a magician's wand pointing to our name. Of course, as with any mother-type effort, we also had tables with pound cake and brownies for sale. And in the center of it all was the Mother's Day card, which drew a steady crowd of signers.

We had set up a speaker's platform, and for the longest time we did nothing but shoot glances at it, wondering when we should—or could—get up there and make our first public statement as a group. It didn't sound like much, but imagine what it's like to be of some considerable age and to be asked to speak at a political rally. Many in our group had no public speaking experience at all. Oh, maybe they had led a church circle or been part of the PTA...but politics? No way. At least not in opposition to the prevailing winds.

We decided to pull out some of the E-mail messages we had received and have the mothers read them to the crowd. Each mother was handed her list and told what her place in the lineup was. We were all so nervous and scared that we sort of clustered together for strength: Eloise and me; Trudy Hogarth; Kay Daughtry; Vernelle Long; Virginia Berger; Pat Johnson; Anne Walker; Eloise's daughter, Rose Vaughn Williams; and the driving force behind the event, Betsy Hunt.

Rose is a beautiful young woman whose heart and spirit shine from her unfiltered. When it was her turn, she spoke of her brother Mark and how she loved him, and told of her pride in her mother's cofounding of MAJIC.

Mel White, author of *Stranger at the Gate: To Be Gay and Christian in America* and a strong human rights advocate, sent a letter that was read to the crowd by a local minister sympathetic to the gay community. (Most recently, White has been instrumental in convincing Jerry Falwell not to attack gay people so viciously.)

Eloise and I spoke last. We explained why we were doing this strange thing, why it mattered so much to us and the other mothers. When we finished, we were both trembling, not from fear but from the sheer desire to be understood. That need remains a driving force to this day for us both.

As the day was closing down, the skies began to darken, and not far off, thunder was warning us to go home. But there was one more event planned: the singing of the "Battle Hymn of the Republic." A young woman named Randa McNamara stood alone under a small grove of trees and sang out, strong and clear, those marshalling words:

"His truth is marching on." Even with the thunder, and the keyboardist playing in the wrong key, I was brought to tears of gratitude and felt a sense of strength that is still with me.

We raced to our cars as lightning cut through the sky. Eloise and I looked at each other as we rolled up the car windows and felt the avalanche of water fall upon us. No turning back now.

Later we looked at the messages on the Mother's Day card, and we knew we couldn't deliver it right away. There was so much that people wanted to say to Jesse, from the serious to the silly to the sublime.

"Your intolerance is intolerable!" one woman wrote.

"May God teach you the real meaning of Christianity!" wrote another.

"Try walking in someone else's shoes for a while."

"Dear Jesse, May you one day find love and compassion in your heart for those people living and dying with AIDS."

"Dear Jesse, Love your hair. Let's do lunch!"

And then there was this, from Rose: "You would have liked my brother Mark."

We may have felt we had stepped into a strange new arena, but we now knew we had many people in the stands cheering us on. The rally garnered us more than $1,600 in donations. Our mailing list swelled into the hundreds. And the card was covered with words we had long thought were only in our broken hearts.

We were official. And we needed help.

The mail alone increased to where I spent every morning on just that. And the donations were coming in. The dreaded quarterly report was approaching, and I hadn't the foggiest idea how to file it. In desperation, I called a young man named Mark Donahue who put us in touch with a CPA who was more than sympathetic to our cause. She came on board with an eagerness we could hardly believe. Now I devoted my mornings to handwriting thank-you notes for our donations.

Shortly before, we had found an enterprising soul to direct our well-intentioned but stumbling actions: Betsy Hunt, a born public-relations type whom I'd met at the AIDS Service Agency. She was extremely feminine and had a marvelous smile but also possessed a will of steel. You couldn't stop her.

Betsy was tenacious, seemed to know everyone or how to get to them, and loved this kind of work. She loved fooling with the big boys and contacting the big media outlets, and she always approached with a disarming, proper manner. But she also cared with a passion about people who were suffering with AIDS and HIV. Betsy already had a full-time job at the AIDS Service Agency, but she said she would work us into her schedule somehow. And she did, with a vengeance. It was she who called *People* and *Time* magazines as well as papers all over the state. It was her friend who led us to the bands that gave concerts for our benefit. Betsy later arranged for a TV commercial to be made and aired. Her energy made the rest of us look like a bunch of sit-by-the-fires.

As is the way of the world, we suddenly needed a staff. The Peter Principle is still in effect, you know. There were T-shirts to deal with, printing to be done, a newsletter to be written, a schedule to keep, and many, many speeches for us to give all over the state.

But all was not coming up roses in our endeavor. The desire to protect what appeared to be one's "turf" reared its dragonlike head. I've always believed and said, "Wherever there are two or three gathered together, there will be dissension." I was right.

Novices we may have been, but shrinking violets we were not. None of us, for that matter. At one point in the campaign, it looked as though MAJIC would go up in smoke. Feelings had been hurt, egos bruised, and resignations tendered. I recall, too vividly, sitting on my bed feeling bereft and thinking it had all been a big mistake and that we should silently fold our tents and steal away. In the midst of my pity party, I was opening the day's mail when I came upon a pizza flyer with a message written on the back.

"Thank you for what you are doing," it said. "I have lost so many friends to AIDS, and I want to help you. Please accept this donation." Enclosed was a check for $5. Tears rolled down my cheeks, and I said aloud, "For you, we can do this."

I, of course, wrote to this young man in Georgia and thanked him, but I doubt if he ever knew what his mailing meant to the campaign.

As our little political foray seemed to be clinging on— even though it was losing ground—a magical phone call came. A local columnist, Nicole Brodeur, called and said *People* magazine was going to run an article about MAJIC and that she was to write the story. I harrumphed into the phone and said there was little MAJIC left.

Nicole just laughed and said, "Oh, it can't be all that bad."

Actually, she was right, but at that moment I couldn't see it. Still, I placed some calls myself with the news that *People* had hopped onto our public relations train, and we were back in business.

As the campaign progressed, we began to attend fundraising events. This was all so new and unfamiliar to us that each invitation was exciting. We were unsure as to what our roles were, but we were willing and anxious to learn.

One event that truly stands out in my memory took place in a garage at the home of two young men who were long-time partners. They had invited a large crowd to their home for the evening, where we were to meet one another, nibble on chips and dip, and talk about the upcoming election.

The night was warm, and the crowd was noisy and jovial. We had an energizing time meeting all these new folks, and as the evening reached the inevitable point where "a few remarks" are made, we wondered if we would be asked to speak. We shouldn't have wondered, but remember, this was still early in the campaign, and we were not yet "old hands" at political activism. Our hosts spoke to the gathering about MAJIC, explaining that we were mothers standing up for gay sons and daughters. When the words, "Let's hear from Patsy and Eloise!" were spoken, we looked at each other with trepidation.

But as we told them of our sons and why we had to act, we could almost feel the warmth of their approval. I'm not sure I remember all that we said, but I do remember a question posed during the informal give-and-take at the end of our remarks. A young man asked in a strong voice, "What advice would you give us in dealing with our parents?"

This could be a hard one. We couldn't speak for all parents, but we could answer for ourselves. And we did.

"Be patient with us," I said. "We diapered you. We rocked you. We loved you then...and we love you now."

It must have been all right, because when we finished, my eye caught the glance of Mitch Foushee, who was leaning against the wall. He gave us a wink and a nod as if to say, *Right on, moms!*

When the evening was over, we were thrilled and surprised to find donations rolling in. That was a generous evening, in many ways.

Within a few weeks we caught the eye of Elizabeth Birch, executive director of the Human Rights Campaign in Washington, D.C. She invited us to speak at the HRC reception at the 1996 Democratic National Convention in Chicago, which would be the high point of our campaign, and one of the high points of our lives.

Eloise hadn't been to a national political convention since 1968, when she'd gone to Chicago with her husband. This time she was headed to the Windy City for her own reasons, but that didn't change her feeling old and out of place.

For me, heading to Chicago was like crossing enemy lines.

Candy Clarke, Mark's sister, wearing a MAJIC T-shirt at the 1996 Names Quilt exhibition in Washington, D.C.

But first things first. Since I wasn't much on clothes, Eloise was afraid I would go to Chicago and embarrass her out of her wits. So she invited me to join her on a shopping trip to the Hudson Belk department store in Raleigh.

"Now, Patsy," she told me, "we're going to go look at some clothes."

I hadn't done any shopping in the 18 months since Mark had died. Basically, I had lost interest in my appearance. There were so many more pressing things to think about, but theater has taught me that whatever we wear ends up being a costume in life's drama. I wanted to be "right" for this daunting trip to Chicago, and I wondered, *Do Democrats dress differently than Republicans?*

Eloise had arranged for a personal shopper to help us at the store, who turned out to be very helpful and patient. At one point, standing in a room walled with mirrors, I caught sight of the rear view. Now, if I hadn't paid any attention to the front for over a year, I sure hadn't noticed the back.

What had happened to my shoulders? One of them was higher than the other. Had I always looked like that? Maybe I was imagining it.

"Eloise, look at my shoulders. Is one of them higher than the other?"

"Of course not." Faithful friend.

"I mean it. Look at them."

"Well," Eloise said hesitantly, "maybe a little."

I made a conscious effort to align them, and it seemed to make the view a bit better. Stress does odd things to us, and since my shoulders are back in the right place now, I can only assume that in "shouldering my burden," I was living in a lopsided manner. But I was leveling the road!

We bought tailored suits to wear in the daytime and silk

suits to wear to our speaking event at the Hyatt Regency Grand Ballroom. My speaking suit was beautifully cut and outlandishly colored—fuchsia! I think it gave me courage, rather like a visual, nonverbal statement: Listen to me! This is important and I will not shrink from saying it!

Eloise chose a two-piece outfit of purple silk, with gold buttons down the front of the jacket. Thinking back, I believe we both chose suits that insisted we be seen and heard. No flowers or pastels this time. We might be grandmothers, but we were leaving our knitting and needlepoint at home.

One summer morning soon after, Eloise and I packed ourselves up. I let her off at the airport curb and went to park the car. There had been so many scares about terrorists then that they didn't even let you into the airport without proper identification. Eloise had packed some extra money and her driver's license into what she called "a private little carrier." Her bra.

As the skycap started to check our baggage, he asked for identification. Eloise turned around, plunged her hand inside her front, and came up with her license. This wouldn't be the only time she did it. Throughout our time in Chicago, she was plunging her hand down her front and acting like it was perfectly appropriate. Who cared?

Once in Chicago, we were invited to several events. At the very first, we learned that talk of the two little grandmothers from North Carolina who were fighting Jesse Helms had made the rounds of the Democratic Party. Of course, that wasn't an entirely good thing. We had hardly sat down to our first breakfast in Chicago before we were tasting exactly what had brought us there—discrimination.

Eloise was especially excited to be at the convention. It was 28 years to the day that she had accompanied her husband, Earl—then speaker of the North Carolina House of Representatives and a delegate—to the DNC in Chicago. It was an experience she would never forget, and despite the controversies swarming around then, Eloise and Earl had had a wonderful time on the floor, at the old Stockyards.

They and the rest of the North Carolina delegation had attended lavish dinners, parties, and brunches at the Yacht Club as the guests of one of the delegation's members, Irwin Belk of Charlotte. Former governor Luther Hodges had been one of the delegates. He had brought along his daughter, Nancy, who was visiting from India. She asked Eloise to accompany her to Marshall Field's, where her father had been president. There, they were given a deluxe tour by a vice president and had a fine lunch in their own dining room.

"I remember I was given my own personalized credit card at the end of the day," Eloise remembered. "Earl used it before we left the city, to buy me the most beautiful dinner suit I had ever seen."

And here she was, back again.

We had been well received at a regular monthly lunch meeting of the Wake County Democratic Women's Club a couple of months earlier. We told them about MAJIC, what we were doing, and how we wanted to help the Democrats win the Senate election. They responded with great applause and encouraged us.

Weeks later we arrived in Chicago, full of confidence. All of the North Carolina Democrats were invited to a large buffet breakfast the first morning, where we saw many old friends and acquaintances. North Carolina Secretary of State Elaine Marshall, several of our state legislators, and some newspeople greeted us. As we took our seats at one of the tables with our juice and muffins, a young man Eloise had seen at the registration desk outside the ballroom, but did not know, came over, sat down, and said, "Mrs. Vaughn, our state chairman asked me to come over to tell you to enjoy your breakfast and please, have some more. But would you please refrain from speaking to members of the press?"

Eloise felt like she had suffered a blow across her face. "We're leaving," she said.

Later, she said, "I was never so hurt in my life. Here at the gathering of my beloved North Carolina Democrats, where I had always felt at home, I was running into the same rejection that Jesse Helms was administering, and for the same reasons: fear and an unwillingness to acknowledge even the existence of a gay-friendly constituency. After all, 'What would people think?' I learned that homophobia, even when cloaked in velvet gloves and delivered with all politeness, abounds everywhere. Even in my own Democratic Party. But that state chairman did us a favor, because the effect on me was 'I'll show you!' It stiffened my resolve, and Patsy and I went on to enjoy the convention and meet more helpful people than we ever thought possible."

Later that day, we listened to a speech by actress Judith Light, who played Ryan White's mother in the television movie about his life. Ms. Light is a great supporter of gay rights, is straight like we are, and believes in the same things we do. Her words grew particularly strong as she spoke to this room filled, for the most part, with gay people: "Don't ask me to go away. I don't care if I'm straight, I am here and I am here to stay."

Eloise and I looked at each other and said, "Same here."

That night we were to deliver our big speech before the national membership of the Human Rights Campaign. We went back to our hotel, put on our new silk suits, and spiffed ourselves up. I even wore earrings, which is the living end for me.

There must have been 1,500 people at the reception. Elizabeth Birch emceed a program that included San Francisco mayor Willie Brown and Sen. Ted Kennedy. I remember watching others before us speak, and also being aware of the murmuring of the crowd and the sound of glasses clinking. In this atmosphere, speeches are secondary.

But when Elizabeth introduced us and we approached the platform, the room suddenly grew quiet. And we began to realize that it wasn't really us—Patsy Clarke and Eloise Vaughn of Raleigh, N.C.—they were listening to. They were listening to the voices of mothers. And we could have been any mothers, fighting those who discriminate against gay people. But we were the fortunate ones who were able to carry that banner.

We talked about our sons. We talked about how they died. We told them about what Jesse Helms said about gay people, and how he fought the funding of AIDS research. We said we were trying to get Helms out before he could hurt any more people like our sons. Like those in the crowd. And like us.

The crowd laughed at the right places. They cried. And they cheered at the end. Eloise said later that if she could get attention like that all the time, she would go back to teaching.

We came off that platform to a line of people waiting to hug us. One woman, we later learned, was a retired anesthesiologist from Puerto Rico and had devoted much of her life to treating AIDS patients.

At one point there was a separation in the crowd—a fortuitous separation. She was maybe 20 feet away from me and our eyes met. Her eyes were so big—I will never forget that. She started toward me, walking very slowly, and it was clear she was coming to me. She got right in front of me, opened her mouth to speak, and nothing came out. I felt like I understood what she was trying to say, and I opened my arms to hug her. When the embrace ended, I felt her tears on my face. I looked at her and said, "I think I understand." She walked away. Never said a word.

Only later did we learn her background: She was a lesbian and a doctor of great accomplishment who had suffered greatly from discrimination. I will never forget her.

After we had spoken and left the stage, Sen. Ted Kennedy and his entourage were ushered up for his speech.

Because I am a recovering Republican, the idea of me, coming from a right-wing background, being on the same platform with Ted Kennedy—even for a moment—was like entering the camp of the enemy. It was a funny feeling but also enlightening. I stood there while Kennedy spoke, marveling at how handsome and well he looked, while Eloise reminded me that he had spoken out and fought for the gay community more than anyone else—save for some gay members of Congress.

As Kennedy left the stage, a man and a woman jumped up and ran onstage, waving pictures of fetuses, shouting obscenities, and making a terrible commotion.

"Senator Kennedy!" the man said. "I have a right to be heard!"

Meanwhile, Elizabeth Birch and someone else—there was no security in the room—were trying to get them both off the stage. We both had a moment of fear because the Kennedys have not had an easy life, and we didn't know whether someone was going to do something awful right there in front of us. Our hearts nearly stopped.

But then Kennedy walked back up the steps, quietly and very dignified, and said, "Yes, you have a right to be heard, and I have a right not to listen." He turned around, walked back down the stairs, and was ushered out of the room.

Other things happened that gave us purpose and comfort.

Eloise connected with a cousin who is a psychologist in Chicago. She told him we were going to speak at the convention, and he came down with his partner and stayed all night. He was a comfort to Eloise, someone from her past. He was very tall and very protective.

We even met one of the first contributors to our campaign, with whom we had only corresponded but never met. But I remembered his name. I even remembered how much he had given, I being so worried about money. He was so pleased.

We returned to Raleigh feeling we had gained political knowledge and political ground. But we needed to stay focused on our greater goal—and somehow, someone always managed to make sure we did.

I remember a call that had lasting and unexpected effects on our efforts. The voice on the other end was a professional acquaintance in the San Diego area, whom I knew only casually. After the customary pleasantries, Steve told me he had a question for me. He said he was HIV-positive, then asked, "Should I tell my mother?"

Now, I had known he was gay, but I did not know he had the virus. As this new and unwelcome knowledge swept over me, my reply came quickly—too quickly: "Of course. You must tell her."

Almost as soon as the words left my mouth, I realized I had no right to say that. I was really speaking for myself, not for Steve's mother. I was saying I wished I had known sooner about my son so that I could have been supportive for a longer period of time. How often we project our own needs onto others.

Immediately, I retracted my words and tried to tell Steve that I couldn't speak for anyone but myself but that I would want to know. On the other hand, I did not know his parents. I did not know what kind of social pressures they lived under. I did not know them well enough to even make an educated guess as to their reaction. He, of course, worried about hurting them and also feared being turned away from them. These are the arrows of HIV, and they are painful.

Steve explained that his mother drove a school bus in the South and his family came from a farming background. They sounded like people who could deal with the basics of life, like loving your children.

Again, I said, "Give her a chance. Tell her."

Steve told me how he had missed being free to converse with his mother about the most important aspects of his life. He loved his family and needed their comfort. As we ended the conversation, I offered to call his mother if he wanted me to. He said he would mull the whole thing over and if he decided to call her he would get back to me.

Not long after, Steve phoned again and said that he had,

indeed, made the call to his mother. While distressed and frightened, she nevertheless expressed the hoped-for acceptance of her son's situation. He asked me to call her and give her another mother's view of the same circumstances. I did. Our talk was brief but full of meaning for me. She was calm, appreciative, and quietly supportive of her son.

"We can handle this," she said. And I know she can.

At this writing, Steve is doing well with the newer AIDS medications, and his stress level is considerably lower since his "secret" is out.

That call made such a difference to Eloise and me because we now had a greater goal than just political effort. We wanted to have a part in a world where no young man would have to call a relative stranger from across the continent and ask, "Should I tell my mother?"

Chapter Seven

THE POWER OF MOTHERS

One of the MAJIC mothers, Trudy, is a retired school secretary in her 70s. She and her late husband had adopted a son, who became prominent in Raleigh before he died. He was a clinical psychologist, an AIDS activist, and a fine man. He was intelligent, had integrity, and was not ashamed of who he was. He had nothing for which he needed to apologize.

At one meeting we got to talking about the power of mothers, and whether we'd succeed in our efforts to get Jesse Helms out of office. After all, we were just a bunch of mothers in flowered dresses and sensible shoes.

"Let me tell you what happened to me once," Trudy said.

She said she was walking to her car at the top of the parking garage at the Crabtree Valley Mall in Raleigh when she heard footsteps behind her. She didn't pay too much attention. It was daylight. She wasn't afraid.

Trudy unlocked her car door, tossed in her pocketbook, and suddenly felt herself being shoved aside. She turned to see a man reaching into her car for her pocketbook. Trudy stood there and with her 70-year-old dignity said, "Your mother wouldn't like this."

The man stopped, took one look at her, and turned and ran—without the purse.

The power of mothers. Everyone has one. Or had one.

That was something we reminded ourselves of throughout the campaign: Everyone who was gay or lesbian or had AIDS or who died of AIDS—every one of those people has or had a mother. What a mighty army, we thought, if we could activate all the mothers. It seemed possible because it seemed so straightforward to us: Stand up for your child, protect your child.

But as we got into this effort, we realized it wasn't going to be that way. We came face-to-face with the power of cultural beliefs, as traditional as candied yams at Thanksgiving. We began to see this different kind of power when Eloise told us the story of a woman from a little town in North Carolina.

Her name was Stella, and it suited her. She was self-assured, slightly rigid, a bit taciturn but outwardly social and friendly. She had two sons, John and James, and they were all part of a prominent family in a small Southern town. Life had been good to Stella, giving her ample material possessions and great security left by her successful and now-deceased husband. She had only to age gracefully and watch her sons do the same. She did not foresee playing a role in the 20th-century drama called AIDS.

The day she received the call from Duke University Medical Center asking that she come to see her very ill son, Stella had no idea what awaited her. She knew Johnny had suffered several attacks of hepatitis, and she presumed this to be yet another. When she reached the hospital reception desk, she was directed to the office of Dr. John Bartlett, someone she had never heard of. He greeted her and told her to sit down. He then told her that her son was terminally ill. He had AIDS.

In the end, they had to restrain her.

"Ma'am," the doctor said, "did you not know that your son is gay?"

Instead of answering his question, Stella—the controlled former Presbyterian elder with the exquisitely coiffed hair and the elegant navy blue dress—leaped to her feet and ran screaming toward the office door. A nurse on the other side of the door grabbed her and held her flailing arms. The doctor rushed over and tried to sit Stella back in the chair. None of these efforts succeeded. Stella possessed the strength of a cornered animal seeking escape. There was no reasoning with such savage emotion, so with great physical effort the two medical workers restrained her, placed her in an isolation room, and waited the fury out.

Stella eventually calmed down outwardly, but she never came to terms with what she had heard that day in Dr. Bartlett's office. She had spent her life with a worldview of respectability that was as unbending as the church pew in which she sat every Sunday. And now her greatest fear was that those who shared that pew would turn from her. She was the mother of a gay son who was dying of the biblical equivalent of leprosy.

Thus began the last 11 months of Johnny's life. When he returned to his home in another North Carolina city,

Stella went with him, and with her went her fear. Fear of exposure, fear of contamination, fear of the loss of the world she knew. It prompted her to take her own sheets and towels to Johnny's house, along with her own dishes and a lot of bleach with which to wash everything.

As Johnny's last days approached, Stella concocted a plan whereby she could keep Johnny's homosexuality a secret. She noticed her son had a young woman friend, divorced and with a child, who faithfully visited and encouraged Johnny. Somehow, in her frantic desperation, Stella was almost successful in convincing this well-meaning young woman to marry Johnny as he lay on his deathbed. Her reasoning (or lack of it) told her that if Johnny's obituary read "survived by his wife," then it would be sad but without the stigma. No one in Stella's unforgiving world would ever know the dreadful truth.

In the midst of this gothic tragedy, the wedding date of Stella's other son, James, was approaching. Not to be deterred by Johnny's imminent death, Stella got him up from his bed and transported him to a store to be fitted for a tuxedo. He couldn't stand, but she had him measured. She insisted that everything was fine and that James's unsuspecting bride must never know the truth of Johnny's condition. If she had to, Stella would prop Johnny up at the wedding because what would people think if the brother wasn't there?

But Johnny outfoxed them all. He died the day before the wedding.

The wedding took place as planned, and Stella convinced herself that her secret was hers alone. Of course, it wasn't.

So that's what we were fighting too, along with Jesse

Helms. We wanted to show mothers like Stella, who were blinded by the fear of losing acceptance, that they weren't alone and that facing the truth could free them to live. We wanted to show children like Johnny that there were mothers who understood and accepted them in their worst days no matter what.

In the course of doing that, the campaign gave birth to several physical icons that demonstrated "the power of mothers."

One of them was that 8-foot-tall Mother's Day card that appeared at our first rally, the one we had decorated with wallpaper that read, LOVE, HOPE, PEACE. All those things that mothers are—at least, that's what we hoped they are. They aren't always.

The power of mothers is also sewn into the Names Project Quilt, which was displayed in Washington, D.C., in October 1996. Eloise and I both had made panels for our Marks, and we wanted to visit this traveling cemetery that honored our sons and so many others.

When it came time for Eloise to consider a quilt square to commemorate Mark Vaughn's life and spirit, Eloise could not, for more than five years, even begin to think of what she could possibly do to capture such a vital life.

"Finally, one night," she told me, "it popped into my head: the strains of Beethoven's Ninth Symphony with the words of Henry Van Dyke, known in the hymn books as 'Joyful, Joyful We Adore Thee.' The third line of the third verse suddenly appeared to be perfect: 'All who live in love are Thine; teach us how to love each other. Lift us to the joy divine.'" Below, on its own staff, with the exact musical notes, Eloise added this quotation: "The music played and then it rested." We also decided to add a full rest at the end of the bar of music. There is no rest in the entire hymn—but there wasn't supposed to be one in Mark's life either.

So Eloise had it. Mark's birth and death dates were set on a rich, blue background—his favorite color. She took the plan to Tony Burden, a professional artist and one of his fellow cast members of *Brigadoon* back in high school. He asked Eloise to bring him a sample of Mark's signature, which he scanned, enlarged, and added above the dates on Mark's panel.

I used the mountains of North Carolina as the backdrop for my son Mark's words, uttered just days before his death:

"This disease is not beating me.
When I draw my last breath
I will have defeated this disease
And
I will be free!"

The original MAJIC mothers posing with their Mother's Day card. From left: Eloise Vaughn, Patsy Clarke, Anne Walker, Trudy Hogarth, JoAnne Harvey, Vernelle Long, Kay Daughtry, and Pat Johnson.

We each sent our panels off to become a part of the vast testament to the suffering and loss of those who had died of AIDS, the symbol of hope for the end of this scourge.

And then, in October 1996, we saw for ourselves how many others had done the same, out of love for their lost one—and how many talented, funny, generous, beautiful people had been taken. At that time, the quilt was made up of 40,000 panels, all of which had been lovingly crafted and offered as a special marker or gravestone. Somehow, the stitches and colors that went into these efforts have a stronger emotional impact than a name etched in granite.

Walking amidst all those panels was an experience I will never forget. The exhibition stretched the entire length of the Mall, and the little walkways between the blocks of panels were crowded with visitors. In that immense arena, you would expect to hear a great deal of human noise—but that was not the case. Reverence hung in the air. When we spoke at all, it was in a whisper. When our eyes met those of a stranger, our sharing was stark. I remember keeping my hand to my mouth almost the entire time, perhaps to stifle any maverick sob that could disturb the quiet.

We found our panels quickly, and after a few moments with them, we looked at others nearby. One in particular stamped itself in my memory: a collage of memories of a lost man. In the center of the panel the maker had laminated a handwritten note dated December 24. It read: "Dear Santa, Give me just a little more time."

Pushing my hand even harder against my mouth, I looked up to see a young man watching me. "He was my partner," he said.

At that, we two strangers hugged each other to mute our sorrow.

Caring for the quilt takes special training and handling. Each morning of the exhibition schedule, the panels were unfolded and put into place in a kind of ritual dance. Onlookers stood at the side, silently watching. All this time, a loudspeaker called the roll of the names represented in the massive monument of fabric. Each one was like the tolling of a church bell.

Unbelievably, I heard "Mark Russell Clarke" called out as the quilt was put into place that early morning. It seemed impossible that I was there at the exact moment they called his name. With so many thousands of names, the process went on all day long. And yet I heard my son's name spoken.

Not only did President and Mrs. Clinton come and

Patsy and Eloise in Washington, D.C., in October 1996, visiting the Names Quilt exhibition. In the background of this symbol of tremendous loss stands the Washington Monument

spend some time walking among the colorful squares, but so did Vice President and Mrs. Gore. It was the first time a president and vice president had viewed the quilt, although it was not the first time it had been displayed on the Mall. One morning Mrs. Gore took a half-hour turn at reading from the long litany of names of all the precious lives represented on the grass. These gestures meant so much to the thousands of us gathered to honor and to grieve.

The quilt is so brave. It flies in the face of cultural stigma, mores, and bigotry. It stitches human beings together instead of ripping them apart.

I wonder if Senator Helms has ever seen the quilt.

As our day ended, Eloise and I decided to walk down to the Ellipse, where the Human Rights Campaign was holding its National Coming Out Day rally. It was getting cold and dark, but we were determined. The other members of our group went back to the hotel. The day had been long and emotionally draining for everyone.

When we neared the meeting site, we realized the event was much bigger than we'd expected. The crowd resembled a state fair without the rides and cotton candy. There must have been 3,000 people milling about.

How we ever spotted someone we knew, I'll never know. But just as we were questioning our good sense at getting into such a crowd at nightfall, we spotted Elizabeth Birch, the executive director of the Human Rights Campaign who had been responsible for taking us to the Democratic National Convention in Chicago.

We called out to her, and her eyes widened with surprise. She said she hadn't known we would be there, or she would have put us on the program to speak. Not being one to hang back, I asked, "What about now? Is it too late?"

I saw Elizabeth consider it. Then she leaned over and told us to work our way to the front, where a fence separated the crowd from the speaker's dais. That way, she said, she would see us and remember that we wanted to speak.

As we wormed our way through the maze of people, I worried that even if we got close, Elizabeth might not notice us, so I pulled out a MAJIC T-shirt with its red, white, and blue logo, draped it over the front of me, and told Eloise to wave at Elizabeth. She did, and Elizabeth saw us.

Soon after, a man came up and said, "Please follow me." We were led through the fence opening to the area behind the speaker's platform. The man said Elizabeth would try to give us a spot in the program, but he cautioned us that we would have only two or three minutes to speak, if that.

The program was filled with interesting people: a leader of NOW, a young woman golfer named Muffin with a great following. And, we were told, Cher was coming.

As the speeches moved along, our guide occasionally touched base with us about the time element. The first time he said Cher was delayed in traffic, and he asked if we could perhaps talk longer if necessary. Of course, I said. When he walked away, Eloise looked at me in a harried way and asked, "What are we going to say?"

"Don't worry," I said. "It'll be all right."

Over the course of more than an hour, the man returned several times with different alerts. We either would have very little time or we would have to span the gap until Cher arrived. We heard regular updates on the progress of her car through D.C. traffic, never really knowing how close she was. As the last speaker was finishing up, we knew we would be next.

Elizabeth got up and said, "And now..." She was getting ready to introduce us, and Eloise and I were both on our feet.

And you know what happened? Cher came.

She was clothed dramatically, in black leather, with bodyguards so big Eloise said they looked like refrigerators.

It's hard to express the feeling in the crowd when she strode to the platform. There was great emotion because Cher's daughter, Chastity Bono, is a lesbian, and Cher had come to stand up for her daughter and others like her.

Everyone cheered and stomped their very cold feet, finally calming down to listen to the short, simple message that came from this mother. I remember especially how casual Cher was, saying something like, "Well, when I first found this out, I didn't really like it, and I didn't understand it, but now...I'm OK about it." And with a shrug of her tiny shoulders, Cher left the platform.

We thought it was all over, and we began looking for exit routes, when we heard Elizabeth say, "We have two mothers who've been waiting through this entire evening to speak to you. I want you to listen to them for a few minutes."

As we were leaping to the steps, Eloise again asked, "What are we going to say?"

"We've done this before and we'll do it again," I told her. "When I turn to you and say, 'Eloise will tell you,' you tell it. Whatever it is."

I talked a bit about the quilt, our sons, and MAJIC. Eloise came in with a punch line and it was over. I don't really remember the words we used, but they must have been all right, because we could feel the response of the crowd, and it was wonderful.

As we descended the steps, a man approached.

"Someone wants to speak with you. Would you come over to the fence?"

We walked over to the fence that separated us from the crowd. And it wasn't some "one" waiting to see us. It was mothers and fathers and brothers and sisters and gay men and lesbians and friends, reaching—so help me God—through the fence. Just reaching. Not only reaching, but thrusting money at us. So much we couldn't hold it. We hugged people through the fence and saw the tears streaming down their faces, especially parents, who said, "Thank you."

We realized it wasn't us they were grateful for. They were grateful that someone was standing up for them and their families. And as much as we appreciated the applause, the hugs, the donations, and the stories of families just like ours, we've always felt sad that people have to be so grateful for simple human decency. Just what we were asking of Jesse.

Mark Vaughn's AIDS Quilt square. The music is from Beethoven's Fifth Symphony, the lyrics by Henry Van Dyke. The hymn is known in the Methodist Hymn Book as "Joyful, Joyful, We Adore Thee."

We must have stood there for half an hour while those folks told us snippets of their own lives and how what we were doing with MAJIC really mattered.

When we finally got ready to go, it was pitch black, so one of the guys from the Human Rights Campaign took us back to the hotel in his car. And as we sat in the backseat, our minds racing with what we had seen and heard that day, Eloise and I looked at each other and knew: If we ever had any doubts about MAJIC, they had been vanquished that night. We now knew for sure that we were doing the right thing. That October night, we realized that our society denied human decency to a whole segment of our population because they do not lead their lives in a way the majority thinks they must.

So society holds back and denies kindness, fairness, and respect, expecting others to follow the cultural lead because it is "the right thing to do." This is standard, staunch conservatism. These are the words, these are the lines. And no one knows them better than I do, because I have recited them. Every one.

But beyond those words and those beliefs, I am a mother. So is Eloise. We are both mothers to four children, one of them gone. We are mothers just like Stella, who denied and bleached and plotted. Our sons' illnesses shocked us too. It caused us to do some measure of damage control. But we found freedom and peace in the truth.

And we are like Trudy, who had been shoved in the mall parking lot. We felt assaulted by Jesse Helms's words and actions. We found a power within us we never knew we had. Every person who assured us, who sent us a check, or thanked us, gave us more strength, like a fresh log on a fire. The stronger that fire got, the more people were drawn to us. They gathered around MAJIC, seeking warmth and light and acceptance—the kinds of things their own mothers, perhaps, never gave them.

Chapter Eight

THE RESPONSE OF OTHERS

My Dear Patsy Clarke,

Just read the article while waiting in my doctor's office and am driven to respond.

You are way off base. You should accept the fact that your son was a biological freak and, as Mr. Helms points out, would probably be here today if he had not played Russian roulette in his sexual activity.

And yes, because of your son's behavior, there are a great number of people, myself included, who feel he was a great deal less than an ordinary individual.

You should open your mind to reality, Mrs. Clarke, and not stew in the juices of a decadent individual.

✳ ✳ ✳

A person for whom I have great respect once said to me, "Everyone hates. You, yourself, have hated."

That simple statement took me aback for a long time. Is that true? Is hate a "natural emotion," or do we confuse anger with hate? Well, the answer will certainly have to come from someone much more erudite than I, but this has certainly occupied much thought on my part, particularly in regard to homophobia, and especially after our campaign started to get press coverage, spurring reactions like the one above, from someone in Oxnard, Calif.

Homophobia has been said to be the "last acceptable prejudice." What a fascinating concept, that prejudice is acceptable. The biblical backdrop most frequently used involves the matter of choice: "You know better, so you must do better."

I remember Mark saying to me with a great deal of sadness seasoned with a touch of bitterness, "Who would choose this?"

Despite the obvious fact that life for a gay person is fraught with more difficulties—and dangers—than for a straight individual, many continue to say it is a choice. Is it rational to believe that a person like Mark Clarke or Mark Vaughn would choose to be afraid of embarrassing their families or, much worse, risk the loss of family love and respect, all for the thrill of a forbidden fruit? And, more importantly, who are we to judge another's relationships, his search for happiness and a true life, things that we all want?

Eloise has said that she felt that her Mark moved away from the city he loved so well because he feared that somehow his homosexuality would be discovered and he would run the risk of hurting his father's career. What an incredible burden for a loving son to shoulder, and all because of a gene that gave him a different direction than his brothers.

I realize people don't always express their true feelings,

but their behavior toward me and the rest of my family was one of caring. For that I am grateful.

I have had the great fortune of being asked to speak at many sociology classes at North Carolina State University. The topic is, most often, "The Effect of AIDS on the Family." These students are so bright and interesting that I have learned far more from them than they have from me. When I face these students, I often wonder how many of them might be gay or have a gay friend or family member. Recent statistics indicate that at least 10% of the population is gay. Almost always, one student asks, "How do you think your husband would have reacted?"

Well, I've asked myself this many times, and all I can say is that I think he would have felt as I do. After all, Mark was his son too, and he valued family over all other considerations. And he certainly was strong enough to stand up for his son as an honorable human being, regardless of any "acceptable prejudice."

Another question that pops up regularly is, "Would you rather that Mark had not been gay?" Well, of course! What mother would want such a difficult life for a child? But that is very different from saying I was ashamed of him. I was not, and I am not now.

I remember a touching moment at NCSU after a class session. It had been a large group, probably 75 students, and this one young man had waited until everyone else had left. He told me had a question he couldn't ask in front of his classmates.

"My brother is gay, and he's in the same situation as your son was," he said. "Tell me how I can help my mom. She's so alone and no one else knows."

What isolation he expressed. And what understanding. I

know I can't tell another person what to do. I can only express what road I've taken and how it's worked for me. Certainly, I've encountered big bumps along the way, but I still think it's been the best path.

I still don't know what hate is, but I have since made a note of an incisive program on PBS whose topic was hate. Bill Moyers and his guests provided many interesting definitions, two that I can't forget: One described hate as "ill will looking for a victim," and another called it "the power to see in others the demons we ourselves create." Scary thought, isn't it?

Eloise and I were given plenty to think about every time we gave a print interview or stood in front of a television camera—and every time we opened the mail or answered the phone, and heard how our quotes and sound bites had been received.

The feedback frightened me at first. My phone would ring and a voice would ask me to comment on something or ask me why we were doing this. Some of these callers were abusive, with an undercurrent of fear in their voice. I remember one man who called and really blasted me. When I asked him who he was, he refused to say, which seemed unfair. After all, he knew who I was. Didn't I have the right to confront my adversary and know his identity? But I discovered the battle we had entered was played by different rules, and I had better get used to them, like it or not.

Until the birth of MAJIC, my press experience had been confined to play reviews and publicity pictures. And Eloise had mostly been at her husband's side. Neither of us expected or knew how to deal with the extensive coverage that came our way. But we realized almost immediately the value of the press in getting our message out. We would accomplish little if we remained a secret. So we became very public.

We got our first taste of wide exposure during our time at the Democratic National Convention, when we were interviewed by Derrick Jackson, a syndicated columnist with *The Boston Globe*. Patient and interested, he questioned us at great length. I was too naïve to realize the opportunity he was giving our campaign. He just seemed like a nice, courteous person who was on our side. When his article came out in the *Globe*, we received calls from news outlets across the country—and with that came donations and great encouragement. We learned that the passion for this cause was much greater than we'd realized or even hoped for, and it came from all areas, in both geography and points of view.

From Chandler, Ariz.: "Dear Mrs. Clarke, There is no doubt in my mind your son Mark is viewing you from above, his heart full of pride and love."

From Chapel Hill, N.C.: "You liberals suck shit. I am glad your sons died. Trust in God."

From Washington, D.C.: "I was raised in New Jersey and vote in Washington, D.C.—but your cause touches people everywhere. Your son would be so proud of you!"

From the Internet: "You plead for people not to be judgmental in one breath and then you go on to use a word like *disgust* in referring to Senator Helms. I'm sure that Helms will defeat Gantt and I'm damned pleased about that prospect! What of the innocent babies and hemophiliacs who have been murdered by the spreading of the AIDS virus? Do you ever consider what these perverts have done and continue doing? And I shouldn't judge? These sexual pigs have killed millions along with the suffering they have wrought. And to top it all off, you ask me to pay for their medical treatment. You people are impossible!"

From Seattle: "I simply wanted to say thank you for being you, and for your hard work. No matter the outcome, you are to be praised and thanked for being a great mom!"

From Denmark: "We have a Danish comic team that appears weekly on TV, commenting on current affairs. At one point, one of them always says, 'I know it's true, because I've said it often.' The same could be said about Mr. Helms."

To our utter amazement, a German paper and the Canadian Broadcasting Company both sent a reporter to interview us. We didn't understand why MAJIC was of interest to anyone other than Americans, but obviously it was.

While I felt we had touched the four corners of the country, and beyond, I remained naïve. Steven Holmes, a reporter for *The New York Times*, called and asked me to tell him about our campaign. I thought he must be a freelancer. We talked a bit, and he was so friendly and encouraging that I thanked him for trying to get us mentioned in such a prestigious paper as the *Times*. "You don't understand," he said. "I *am The New York Times*."

He sure enough was, because shortly after, on October 1, 1996, the *Times* printed an item in its Political Briefing section with the headline, "Mothers Organize to Oppose Helms."

"As interest groups go, it is small and underfinanced," the article began, "and its leaders harbor no illusions that they will have much impact on the Senate race in North Carolina. But that matters little to Mothers Against Jesse in Congress..."

The article noted that we didn't have much money, only about $15,000, and that we had two part-time workers and a few volunteers working from a card table and chair in my bedroom, and a fax machine and desk in Eloise's study.

"It's a mission," Mr. Holmes quoted me. "It has to be done. My eyes have been opened to much injustice, much bigotry, and much hatred. I can no longer, with my very, very comfortable life, just hold my tongue and do my knitting and my needlepoint."

On November 4, we were profiled in *People* magazine, which also generated a lot of donations and response. In the article, Jack Betts, an associate editor at *The Charlotte Observer*, told *People* we had "the same credentials as Jesse's voters do. They are not from somewhere else, and they are saying, 'My family has diversity: someone who is divorced or gay or on welfare.' They may have some impact."

All of this exposure and reassurance prepared us for our most aggressive move of the campaign.

One day Betsy Hunt called and said, "I have a professional who wants to make a TV ad for MAJIC."

At that point, the amount of publicity was becoming almost more than I could bear. People who had known me in the past were looking at me like I had lost my marbles. The thought of a TV commercial that thousands of people would see was frightening. Oh, I know we had said from the beginning that it was one of our aims, but I never thought we'd get enough money in the pickle jar to pay for it. It seemed a wonderful and safe fantasy.

And now Betsy was telling us it could be real. My luke-warm reception rolled right over her, and she set everything up for an evening hour at Eloise's house, on the sunporch, where so much of our work had taken place.

The night arrived, and the place was an absolute hive of activity. The "real stuff" of making a TV ad was all there: lots and lots of wires all over the floor, big overhead lights, and, of course, cameras. A director, a sound technician, and an assistant type conferred with one another while we mothers stood by, mouths agape. We had our customary Sunday clothes on and did silly things like tearing up the Kleenex clutched in our hands or saying, "I'm going to the restroom. I'll be right back" and "Is my hair all right?"

When they were ready to shoot, they looked at us and said, "Now, we don't have a prepared script. We're just going to let you mothers talk a bit, and we'll work what you say into something else, which we have prepared."

Panic! What would we say? Most of the group had never faced a television camera, and hadn't the foggiest notion of what was expected. Charles, the wonderful man in charge of the commercial, told us to take turns speaking out and saying something we wished we could say to Jesse Helms. That bit of advice helped, because each mother had something that mattered especially to her.

I was last, and I truly felt I would not have a sound to utter. But as I listened to those women who had become my friends under such intense circumstances, I felt again the reasons we were doing what we were.

As the mother next to me finished, and I knew I was the last remaining, the words just fell out of my mouth: "Oh, Jesse."

The sadness that I felt for all of us washed over me. Not just for our sons, or ourselves, but for Jesse and those who believe that our sons were less than human. When those two words were uttered, the sunroom grew very still. The cameras stopped, and I knew that those two words were spoken on behalf of all mothers and fathers of gay sons and daughters. It felt like a prayer.

And so, not long after, we gathered again at Eloise's with our close friends and supporters, and watched the tape.

The ad opens with a black screen and a drumbeat playing in the background. As the camera moves back to show the mouth, and finally the full face of Jesse Helms speaking into a microphone, lines of text are displayed on the screen.

"For 24 years, this mouth has spewed distortions, half-truths, and intolerance," the first one reads. "It has told the less fortunate that they need no help. It has told the bereaved that they need no comfort. It could unify. Instead it divides. It could have been a force for good. Instead it appeals to the worst in all of us. To gain 50.1% of the vote, he has behaved badly and made rude remarks."

Once the full image of Jesse is clear, the ad cuts to five of the MAJIC mothers, sitting and standing, stone-faced and frowning.

I shake my head like the disappointed mother I am, and intone, "Oh, Jesse."

He would give me more reasons to say that in the days to come.

Soon after, we were featured in *Time* magazine, under the headline: "Mothers Know Best?" The item detailed the commercial and its script, specifically where we chastise Jesse for "distortions, half-truths, and intolerance."

"Not words Helms wants to hear," the article said. "MAJIC believes he has ensured that most North Carolinians won't hear them either. Of eight stations approached by MAJIC, only three agreed to run the ad. Others begged off on 'content' or said they didn't have time."

"We know that Helms has threatened to sue a number of stations if they air our spots," Betsy was quoted in *Time*.

It turned out that Jesse's campaign had claimed that

MAJIC was not a legally registered PAC, even though it was, and that a member of an advertising agency working for Helms said WRAL in Raleigh would be "in trouble" if it ran the ad. WRAL conferred with its lawyer and aired the spot anyway.

In the midst of all this, a local television reporter, Amanda Lamb, interviewed us about our status with the Federal Election Commission and then went to Helms to give him the chance to respond.

Apparently, Jesse didn't have much to say about his people suspecting us of not being a legally registered PAC. We were not worthy of concern—even though we had recently appeared on a list of 14 "ultra-left, fringe, special-interest groups out to smear Jesse Helms and help Harvey Gantt." MAJIC was third, behind N.C. Mobilization '96 and an affiliate of the AFL-CIO.

But Amanda Lamb stood there waving a roll of papers at Helms, saying her station had checked with the FEC and, indeed, all of our filings were up to date. I can't express what it meant to me to have an objective source say we were legal, especially since we had tried so hard to fill out the forms and get them in on time. Believe me, if you think the Internal Revenue Service makes life difficult, just try to understand FEC regulations. Their bulletin was my bedtime reading for months. To think that some opposing group could not even credit us with trying to do the right thing—what a discussion that would have made at the old round table.

No wonder we welcomed the chance to do several very diverse radio interviews. Two remain strong in my mind because they were out of San Francisco. I'd had no idea how many people listened to talk radio in that area, because after both of those radio programs the phones in our homes rang, and the letters came—letters filled with money. And not just $5 donations; some were $100. I know it doesn't sound like much when we think about what Senator Helms raised, but it was a lot to us.

At the end of each radio show was a call-in segment. The response was unbelievable, and it kept on for a long time.

We went on another radio program in Charlotte. It aired at midnight, which was hard for Eloise and me, because both of us go to bed with the chickens. But we stayed up that night and drank a lot of coffee.

The radio station informed us in advance that the host was a liberal talk-man, so we felt quite confident that he'd be on our side and that we wouldn't have to face difficult questions. That was fine; at midnight we didn't need difficult questions.

The host was indeed nice, and some pretty hateful calls did come in. He would always say, "Just let me handle this, ladies," and then he'd take over, because he felt so strongly about our position. He wanted to protect us. I appreciated that. And so did Eloise.

At the end of the program, he said, "Well, Patsy, would you say that Senator Helms is just mean—or stupid?"

And I listened to that, and I thought, wait a minute. Thank heaven I did.

"Now, that's asking me to make a judgment," I said. "And that's exactly what we're railing against. I can only tell you that I dislike and detest and disagree with the stance Senator Helms has taken on these issues. But I can't judge him as a human being. I don't want him to judge my son or other people like him."

The guy was so nice. He said, "Hmm. You've given me something to think about."

I felt really good about that.

We appeared on another talk show, out of Wilmington, N.C. Eloise took care of that one, since I'm not as good on the Bible as she is. We were talking, both taking turns answering questions, and the host was absolutely against us. But he wanted us on because we made people angry, so that was good for his business.

The host took the first caller's question: "I would like to ask Mrs. Clarke this: Are you a Christian?"

I looked at Eloise and knew the expected answer. I knew my own answer.

"Well, yes. I consider myself a Christian."

Note: I said, "I *consider* myself a Christian."

I didn't say this, but I'm quite confident that the person asking the question would not consider me a Christian. But I see myself as a Christian. And it's OK if someone disagrees with me, but he has no right to tell me whether I am or am not. I decide that.

Well, we went on with the program, and someone else called in and asked, "What do you say about the verse in Ezekiel," number such and such?

And I must confess, I'm not well versed in Ezekiel. I pretty much know about Genesis and Matthew, Mark, Luke, and John. A little about Exodus. But Ezekiel, I drew a blank. I looked at Eloise, and she knew I was floundering.

"Well," she said, "I think I can deal with that."

She handled it absolutely perfectly. It was wonderful. Took care of it completely.

After the program ended, Eloise's son Stuart, who lives in Wilmington, called her up and said, "Mom, I happened to tune in. Don't ever get yourself in such a position again!"

Exposing your deepest thoughts and beliefs in the public eye does test your mettle. It makes you aware of how people try to trap you. But we held our own, thank God and our boys.

* * *

Ever since I received that hateful missive from Oxnard, Calif., I've wanted to answer the writer. But because it was unsigned, I could not reply.

Now I can.

To the anonymous writer in Oxnard, Calif.:

Your letter reached me right after the election. Obviously, the article in *People* magazine really stirred you up, as you felt "driven to respond" to it.

Yes, hate and fear are strong motivators. I wonder if you've thought about the mother who was to receive your virulent thoughts? Did you fantasize about my reaction? Did you think, "I really told her!"? And, safe behind your anonymity, you could never really know. Until now.

Let me tell you what it's like to receive a letter like yours. I always opened the mail in my bedroom. I had a makeshift desk in there where I wrote the thank-you notes to people who encouraged our campaign against the senator. The great majority of letters were supportive and gave me a lift for the day's activities.

The day your letter came, I happened to be sitting on my bed reading and sorting through the mail.

The election was over, and I was wondering if it had been worth it...all the effort, the tensions, the inevitable human conflicts. And then I opened your letter and read that I should face the fact that my son was "a biological freak."

Well, Anonymous Writer, my son was not "a biological freak." He was an academically gifted, very handsome, very tall (6 foot 7) individual, and had more charm than was good for him. At the time of his HIV diagnosis, he was a law student. And he would never have presumed to call another human being "a biological freak." I taught him better than that.

You advised me to "face reality" and to "stop stewing in the juices of a decadent individual."

There was nothing decadent about Mark Clarke. He went to Sunday school, was a Cub scout, acted in plays, and volunteered at a hospital. He was the youngest in a family of four children and was much loved by all of us.

Mark only lived to be 31, but in those years he brought a great deal of joy to many people. His interactions with his fellow human beings brought smiles, more often than not. Never would he have designated another as a biological freak.

As I write this, I feel again the outrage and sense of helplessness I felt on that cold November day. The election was over, and your brand of thinking had won again. What was the point of it all?

And then my eyes fell on the pile of letters from which yours had come. Every one of them said, "Keep on!" I saw a picture of my son smiling at me across the room. I remember hearing the sound of my own voice saying, "Well, if this is who's against us, then we're surely on the right side!"

And now, as I write this, I still want to shout at you, whoever you are, "What gives you the right to judge my son?"

But a stronger, quieter voice within me says, "Thank you for exposing the evil in our midst. Thank you for making me want to continue this fight against bigotry. Thank you for showing me the face of fear. Somewhere I've I learned that evil exposed is two thirds destroyed."

So watch out, Anonymous Writer. We won't give up.

Chapter Nine

AFTER THE ELECTION

Election night came. How to explain my concept of inevitability? We had always known that the challenge we had taken on would not succeed, in the ordinary sense of the word. But even if failure was inevitable, our effort was just as inevitable. We had to try. We had to stand up. We had to keep singing, even if we felt unheard.

We had all voted, wearing our MAJIC buttons at our various polling places. By this time we'd grown used to the stares and occasional comments about our efforts. Mostly we heard "Right on!" and "Keep it up!" Friends buoyed our outlook, but deep down we knew our victory would not be found at the polls. Oh, we hoped, of course. We often referred to the story of David and Goliath, hoping that our small stone of effort could hit the mark.

But it was not to be. That night, when the count was being tallied and we realized our loss would be actuality and not speculation, we faced a monumental letdown.

We had gathered at Eloise's home, where she had arranged a great display of food to feed our sagging spirits. Dressed in our best, so as to help feel our best, we greeted our supporters of the past months. I wore my gold AIDS ribbon pin. It had been a gift from Mark, who'd given it to me the first Christmas after he told me he had AIDS. And while I had learned so much, so fast that year, I didn't know what the pin signified when I first opened the box.

"Mark, it's very pretty," I'd said. "What does it mean?"

He looked at me with an expression that asked, *How can you not know what this signifies?* And I truly didn't. Hard to believe now that I was so unaware of the symbol of the disease that would take my son from me.

Mark explained that by wearing the ribbons, people showed their support for finding a cure for AIDS.

"I hope you'll wear it," he said wistfully.

It is like a monument now. It is glued to me.

As election night progressed, we talked among ourselves and buoyed one another with hopeful remarks. Early in the evening, our voices were strong and easily heard, but as a bit of time passed, they grew more muted and indistinguishable. Just below the surface, we knew we had lost. How could we win when we faced a political giant? We were truly a small voice in the wilderness.

As the polls closed and the TV stations aired their projected winners, we knew it was over. No long, suspenseful night for us. Jesse Helms was reelected.

We said the things losers say to one another: "Well, we tried" and "We gave it our best effort" and "We would do it all again."

One young gay woman sat on the floor beside her mother, who was rocking slowly back and forth in her chair. The

140

daughter patted her mother's knee. Funny, isn't it? A reversal of roles.

Eloise and I didn't say anything to each other. There was no need. It would have just been excess verbiage. We knew. We knew it like we knew it was Tuesday. You know the look that passes between two people who know what's going to happen? That's what passed between us.

As people collected their coats and sweaters, preparing to go, Mitch Foushee asked if I would go to another gathering of supporters and say a few words. Eloise had to stay because she was the hostess in her home, so I went alone.

At that gathering, the mood was even more somber. Like Sisyphus, we had pushed the stone part way up the hill, only to have it fall back on us. As I stood there with them, it felt like we had all failed one another.

But as the words came, I found myself saying we hadn't lost. Looking at their faces, I knew they thought I was just mouthing a cliché. To my own surprise, I meant it.

We really hadn't lost, because we had spoken out against what we considered an injustice. Susan B. Anthony used to say "Failure is impossible," and I think she was right. Entrenched fear can be spaded up and new ground broken. Maybe we had taken part in plowing some fresh furrows.

As Eloise put it, "The campaign opened my eyes and opened my heart to a new purpose, and that is to help other people. I have a lot to do for the rest of my life, and Jesse is just a small part. We never really thought we could bring down Jesse Helms, but we had the satisfaction of knowing we did make a statement. We are confident and satisfied that we made a statement, and that was to say to politicians, 'It isn't right to talk this way. It isn't right to use my son as a means to an end—that end being the attainment of power through prejudice.' That gave us a lot of comfort, and that is what I take away from that year. To my dying day, the MAJIC campaign will be one of the most satisfying things I have ever done."

It took a little time for us to come to that realization. For several weeks after the election, we struggled to boost ourselves and each other up. At some moments we felt like we had wasted our efforts.

And we still had a lot of mail to open—a "mixed bag" if there ever was one.

From Chapel Hill: "Looks like your little crusade didn't work. Ha, ha, ha."

From Boston: "Even though it made me real sad to see that Helms won reelection, I can only imagine the disappointment you must be feeling. I can only appreciate the hard work that your organization has done to enlighten people with love and understanding, to counteract the hate in the world. Even though he won again, it is important what you attempted to achieve, and this does not mean it is all over with. The struggle goes on, and it is important that we have people like you and Mrs. Vaughn in the world. As a gay man who also happens to work in AIDS services, it is so incredibly refreshing to know that there are mothers like you in our world. I know that Mark is looking down on you with so much pride and joy. Keep up the work."

Indeed, we found that we were still the MAJIC mothers, and always would be. The friendships, the knowledge, and the perspective we had gained during the campaign informed everything we did beyond November 1996.

When Mark Vaughn died, Eloise reacted by finding

others like herself and talking about their grief—but not her own. Then we met and found the common misery that activated us both. With that, our worlds began to shake, as I experienced a political earthquake and Eloise a spiritual one. In the early days of the campaign, the tremors were relatively mild, but as we worked through those days, the split in the earth felt irrevocable; new continents were formed in our thinking, and in our hearts.

For Eloise, that created a change in her relationship with her church. Raising her voice as one of the founding members of MAJIC made it easier for her to speak her mind in the one place she never really had. A few have joined her, but condemnation is much easier. It is much easier to join the choir of voices singing "Everybody knows..." than to venture a solo with an unfamiliar tune.

So, here we include some of Eloise's thoughts on why she wants to stay in her church. And even though I don't understand that desire, I applaud her strength. I envy her, really, because she still hopes.

✳ ✳ ✳

It started one summer Sunday many years ago. My children and I had all gone to the big downtown Methodist church for Sunday school and for the main service. My husband was away on business, but the children and I were all where we were supposed to be on a Sunday morning. And now, dinner had ended and the sultry, resting time of the Sabbath had come.

I was upstairs changing into my easy clothes when I heard the first sound. It started low, like a moan, and then built in volume, and in agony. By the time I reached the stairs and ran down, searching for the source of the sound, it had become a howl of pain. I ran into the dining room and saw my son Mark, doubled over with the power of the noise emanating from him. Tears streamed down his face, and I took him in my arms and murmured the sounds that mothers have made since the beginning of time.

My frightened adolescent boy, who didn't even know the meaning of what he was about to tell me, took a breath and gasped, "Mr. Pickett called me a queer!"

When the emotional storm had subsided, and I was able to get Mark to stop crying, I talked with him the very best I could. But I was only a young woman in my 30s. I couldn't believe that this incredible emotional injury had been inflicted upon my firstborn—and by his Sunday school teacher, at that.

How could I explain what the accusation meant? How could I explain that it came from a representative of God's church, whose primary tenet was to love one another? It was one of my first experiences in dealing with man's inhumanity toward his fellow man.

After an hour or more had passed and both Mark and I were completely drained, he went to his room to do whatever a 12-year-old does to repair his emotional well-being. And I sat on a step halfway down the staircase, hugging my knees close and rocking back and forth.

When I remember this time in my life, I am always taken aback by the knowledge that some of my greatest hurts have come at the hands of those who profess the greatest kindness: pillars of the church.

I've always felt that I had big things to do, things I had to accomplish. I think I developed a certain audacity and larger-than-life desire to do and to be. I learned to be passionate in these desires and to be and do my best. The church had much to do with this. I believed in its teachings to work with others for the good of all. I was then, and still am, an optimist.

I had always believed in the basic goodness of people, which is why I was so surprised and shocked and hurt when I discovered this was not always the case in regard to people who had AIDS and people who were gay. I just could not understand the mean-spiritedness of people, especially people in leadership roles in society and, particularly, in the church. I expected the best from them.

I was first taken to the Methodist church when I was an infant, and I continued to be a part of the programs of the church on through regular Sunday school, summer Bible school, and teenage Methodist Youth Fellowship. It was also great fun to help my mother when she held circle meetings in our homes. We helped serve refreshments at the conclusion of the program. I was one of the girls in the church who helped our mothers serve hearty country ham and vegetable "suppers" to the civic clubs who happily came out from town for a sat-isfying evening in the country. The money raised from these suppers went a long way toward meeting church expenses. After we had helped prepare the meal, we slipped into a back Sunday school classroom, changed into our Sunday best, and became "servers."

After college and my marriage in 1952, we moved to a small town in north central North Carolina. Our four chil-dren were baptized, and they participated in similar church activities, including the scouting program.

I will always remember their singing wonderful songs with lyrics such as "Red and yellow, black and white, they are precious in his sight. Jesus loves the little children of the world." And I thought, yes, the church is teaching them the great tenets of the faith, just as it taught me. They are learning from the same wellspring of the church from which I learned.

At their baptisms, the minister held them in his arms and assured us and the congregation that "the lives of these precious children are all blessed in the sight of God." Years later, after I learned that my firstborn child was gay, after I began to realize how many of my friends and my friends' children were gay, and after I found that the church did not feel the same toward these "precious children of God" despite its protestations that they "loved the sinner, hated the sin," I developed strong doubts about the proclaimed faith in which I had sought solace, comfort, and strength all my life.

Another of my sons whispered to me one morning during such a service a couple of years ago, when the minister stated how God loved each and every one of these children, "Yes, unless they turn out to be gay."

While I was serving on the administrative board of the church (membership was around 3,000), its official publishing house printed a study program called "The Church Studies Homosexuality." The program was taught in one of our Sunday school classes, and some of the members volunteered to teach it to others. Based on a three-year study conducted by a committee drawn from the fields of psychology, religion, ethics, and medicine, it was not a perfect program, but it was enough to open minds and promote deeper thinking about the treatment by the church of its homosexual, transgendered, and bisexual members.

Just as the letter from Jesse Helms set Patsy off on a new journey—and a painful one, in which she questioned long-held beliefs and made painful but true decisions—this study spurred me into action.

146

Two years earlier, the Metropolitan Community Church, which ministers to lesbians and gays, joined the ecumenical ranks of the North Carolina Conference of Churches. This organization, which serves as an umbrella of many denominations in eastern North Carolina, accepted this church's money. This enraged the Methodist churches in the area, so they voted at their annual conference to implement economic power and withhold their financial support of the NCCC. Ironically, the Methodist church had helped start the NCCC in the 1930s so that churches could work together to aid the orphaned and homeless—those who had been marginalized by society.

Realizing that my own local church felt stigmatized by any association with a "gay and lesbian" church, I got up at a monthly meeting of the administrative board and proposed that it promote this study of homosexuality within our own church, using the materials that the denomination had already approved. That way, I argued, when the matter of the Metropolitan Community Church's membership in the NCCC came up again, our delegates to the conference would be informed. Better yet, we would say to the world—and particularly to our gay and lesbian members—that the church truly loves all of God's precious children.

That night, I had very few supporters. An openly gay man seconded my proposal and a supportive psychiatrist spoke in favor of it. Of the 50 or so other members in attendance, not one supported my proposal. Many rose to castigate the whole idea and to add their voices to those who believed that "encouraging" the homosexuality study was wrong.

Later, an internal church study was done surrounding this issue, and, after it was presented, the administrative board passed a resolution to restore funding to the NCCC, and agreed it would take the resolution to the regional conference. There, in June 1996, the resolution was presented—and the senior pastor of my church spoke against it. That, to me, was amazing.

Today, the Methodist churches of eastern North Carolina still refuse to be part of the NCCC—all to show their disdain and disapproval for a little church they deem "unclean." I know the Methodist Church welcomes gays if those "lost souls" enter one of the "ex-gay" programs. To it, being gay is a matter of choice that prayer and study can change, and unless a gay person undergoes such a change, he or she is still outside the pale.

When I think of these people, I think of that H.L. Mencken maxim: "There is always an easy solution to every human problem—neat, plausible, and wrong." My own minister is among the leaders of this group. I keep thinking, where is simple brotherly love?

More than ever, I question whether what I was clinging to was, after all, hollow. What had appeared to me as a bulwark of strength and assurance belied its appearance. Could it be that it dressed itself in the robes of spirituality, but when bared, it bore the scars of prejudice? If I had to leave the church, where would I go?

I see a critical mass building toward a brighter future. And unwillingness to learn more about what we don't understand is willful ignorance. If I drive down the highway going 80 mph in a 55 mph zone, I cannot plead with the highway patrolman who stops me, "Officer, I didn't know it was wrong." That would be willful ignorance.

There are so many signs along our way now, so much good information all around us, that to deliberately ignore it or purposefully turn our backs is willful ignorance. I understand *fear, and I realize that a lot of what we hear coming from church people and others is fear—of the unknown, of change, of the opinion of others.*

It reminds me of a quote from Eric L. Harry's book, Society of the Mind: *"Whenever you try to change people's beliefs, you are in for a real fight. There's a reason we say old ideas die hard. It's because they have to die. And what kills them is a better idea. A more believable idea."*

When Mark was sick upstairs in my home for 18 months, I asked again and again for my former pastor to come see him. Mark talked to me all the time about how he had never felt a part of the church, not since childhood. He had many questions for me about life, dying, death, and reconciliation. I did not want my dying son to think that he—who had always been so caring of others and so careful to extend a hand of friendship—was of no concern to the church he had joined at age 12.

I did not feel that I'd received adequate care or concern from my church. Even after Mark's death, there were no calls or visits, not even a pat on the shoulder when I did return to services. Not long after Mark's death, a couple in the Sunday school class I attended gave the altar flowers in memory of two other people's sons who had died of other causes. The omission was conspicuous to me, and it hurt. I felt that Mark's death didn't count in their minds. This is not to say they were overtly unkind to me. Maybe they just didn't know how to comfort me. Perhaps willful ignorance held sway again.

I no longer wanted to go to hear what now sounds like empty platitudes from the pulpit. How could this be the church that taught me that all God's children are "precious in his sight"? As a hopeful and optimistic person, I want to believe that a new spirit will come upon our people. We are being lead to a higher consciousness. And I have to remember that the leaders in this new spirit, now regarded as heretics, eccentrics, and worse, will be recognized in time as visionaries, saints, and modern-day prophets.

I have met so many of them: selfless, dedicated, risk-taking people. Their lives have been totally immersed in the twin works of caring for those sick with AIDS and trying to find a cure, and working to fight blind hate, harassment, and marginalization. Many times they are "straight" themselves but still recognize the two-headed monster of prejudice and bigotry for what it is, and, as in the civil rights movement of the '60s, throw their all into the struggle.

There are doctors and researchers, such as Dr. John Bartlett, director of the HIV clinic at Duke University Medical Center.

There are people who run AIDS care agencies, who feed the hungry and try to heal the sick.

There are the novelists and playwrights, such as Tony Kushner, author of Angels in America, *who bring the reality of AIDS to the people.*

There are visionary media people taking brave stands.

There are movie stars, such as Judith Light, who, after playing the part of Ryan White's mother in the TV movie, found herself permanently committed to help us fight all the injustice involved with this issue.

And, of course, there are those who carry the virus.

* * *

In June 1997, we were asked to ride in the gay pride parade in Carrboro. This kind of event is a more flamboyant aspect of the gay and lesbian rights movement, and even though I had come a long way in standing up publicly, this invitation seemed a bit too far out for me. I wanted to weasel out of it, but Eloise said we must do this.

Putting my more cowardly instincts aside, I agreed, and sure enough, we showed up at the appointed time to be the grand marshals for the parade. Our chariot was a vintage pink Cadillac. Probably the first and last time I ever rode in one. True to the flamboyant nature of the event, we clambered up onto the top of the backseat (it was, of course, an open convertible), and sitting as high as the vehicle would allow, we perched unsteadily as the car started its long, slow trail through the crowd.

We saw faces we recognized. We waved. People shouted and called out, and then we really got into the spirit of the day. Blowing kisses and waving, we finished out the course. I never learned the "queen wave," so my hands ached when it was over.

Perhaps our most meaningful moment came in February 1997, when we received the Human Rights Campaign's Equality Award for our work with MAJIC.

I attended the banquet in Greensboro that night. Eloise was returning from a trip to Australia, winging her way across the ocean.

By now, I should have been used to the huge crowds at such events. In my less than knowledgeable days, I had assumed that gays and lesbians made up a very small percentage of the population. The 1996 campaign had educated me otherwise. While still a minority, gays and lesbians are a large minority.

Another aspect of this new experience was my own, somewhat uncomfortable, awareness of being a minority myself. There I was, a straight grandmother in a ballroom full of folks I had been taught to view as odd. But they weren't. They were just like any other group I found myself in. The only difference was the nature of their cause.

Recalling this event reminds me of an exchange I recently had with a man who was about my age. We were both in a class called "Thinking About Politics" at the Encore Center, part of a program sponsored by North Carolina State University that offers enrichment classes for senior adults. I had mentioned the work I do on behalf of gays and lesbians. He politely and quietly asked if he could pose a personal question. I said yes, and braced myself for the "How *can* you?" type of inquiry.

But I relaxed as he asked, "Was it hard for you?"

Now, that question could contain much hidden subtext, and I knew it.

"Do you mean, was it hard that my son was dying, or that he was gay?"

"That he was gay."

"Well," I began, "since the train was rushing full speed toward me, I didn't have time to consider a cultural reaction to the reality of a devastating loss. So, no, it wasn't hard that he was gay. It was horrible that he was dying."

Feeling that one question deserved another, I turned the tables on him.

"May I ask you a personal question?"

"Of course," he said.

"Why do you ask?"

"Well, in my younger days," he said, "I thought they were promiscuous and—"

I interrupted, as I am inclined to do. "You mean like heterosexuals?"

He looked at me with great good humor and said, "Yes, but I didn't have the maturity to recognize that at the time. But later I came to have some friends who were gay, and I found them to be just...people...like the rest of us."

A simple conversation but brimming with truth. Just people. Like the rest of us.

I thought of that conversation as I sat at the HRC banquet. As with all banquets, many speakers were offering citations and recognition. We were just another group among many, but when Mitch Foushee went to the dais to introduce our award, I felt my breath suspended. I watched that wonderful man, who was even then so ill, stand there and thank Eloise and me for what we had done. In reality, he was thanking us for human decency. And I wondered, why would there be an award for that? It made me realize that civil rights are human rights.

When Mitch signaled for me to respond at the platform, I suddenly felt awed and speechless. Looking at those upturned faces, with big smiles and open expressions, brought the memory of the past months and effort back in a rush. I wished that our Marks could have been in that assemblage, knowing that their mothers were supporting them in the face of the world. But they had to die before we did that.

"Those of you who know me know I am seldom without words," I began. "Translated, that means I talk too much. But tonight I find myself with very little to say, except thank you, and, to recall what someone said to me early on in the campaign: 'I understand how you feel, but do you have to wear it like a badge?' I answered, 'Yes, I have to wear it like a badge, because I can. And I see it as a badge of honor.'"

As I made my way back to my table, my eyes met my daughter Candy's, and she gave me a great big smile as she held out my chair.

It was a spectacular evening, one I remember every time I look at the clear blue crystal award sitting on my bookshelf.

May my eyes always be as clear to see the truth.

Chapter Ten

THE POSITIVE SIDE
AND THE THINGS WE CAN'T EXPLAIN

While the MAJIC campaign didn't reach its goal of unseating Jesse Helms, it perhaps found a greater goal, and greater success, in bringing out the stories of parents, families, and loved ones who responded in a positive way to those who have come out of the closet, and those who have AIDS.

The first stories we heard came from the women who were the heart and soul of Mothers Against Jesse in Congress. Others came from people we met at rallies, at fund-raisers, in bars and backyards. We received testimonials in the mail, wrapped around campaign contributions, and over the Internet and telephone. Every time we grew weary from the fight or our spirits flagged, there came a story of a mother like us, or a son like our Marks, to revive us and renew our resolve.

We only started listening—really listening—when our

sons told us they were HIV-positive. It's strange that something so awful could be described that way at all. So here we offer our own kind of "positive." Positive stories with a message that we could never ignore: Love transcends religion and politics, time and distance, peer pressure and prejudice.

One day during the campaign, Eloise received a letter from Catherine Cameron of Siler City, N.C. She was unable to be active in the MAJIC movement, but she wanted to share with us an essay she had written. Her words moved us on their own, but did even more so when we learned that Catherine's husband, Angus, is a retired United Methodist minister who was ordained and served in the parish ministry for more than 40 years.

The Person God Intended Him to Be

It will stay forever in my memory as a special day because it held, for me, sudden understanding. A dawning.

Paul, the younger of our two sons, now graduated from college and working in Durham, was home for the weekend.

"Mom, are you busy?" he asked one Sunday afternoon.

"Well, I thought I might go to the Chatham Historical Society meeting," I said. "It's here at the church this afternoon...but I don't have to go."

"Could we go for a walk, then? I'd like to talk with you."

We started down the street by the parsonage, cut across the lawn below the cemetery, and found ourselves seated under a large old tree. There, Paul told me what was on his mind, very simply and honestly.

"I'm a homosexual," he said.

How had I not known? In all those 26 years, how had I not become aware? Now, in one brief moment, so many things fell into place.

But first, first... "Paul, when did you know?"

"When I was in my early teens," he said, "I realized I was different from the other kids. It was as if a huge black hole opened up in my life."

I was weeping now, in agony, for this son, this perceptive, compassionate, shy person. This lonely, self-effacing, often angry person. He had gone through those adolescent torments alone. If only I had known.

My husband, Angus, and I had tried to understand, tried to help. We had encouraged and supported as best we knew, but still, we could see that as a teenager and even in college, Paul had often seemed remote, unable to focus in order to use his talents to the fullest, unable to realize and appreciate his attractive attributes.

I had noticed in the past few months, though, that he had seemed less tense, more outgoing and self-assured. Now he explained that, after years of private struggle and despair, he had finally gone to a counselor to ask for help in changing his sexual orientation. The counselor said he could not change Paul's sexuality but assured him that he would listen and support him in his quest for discovery and growth.

Feelings of gratitude toward that counselor surged through my heart and mind, and do so even as I write. How fortunate Paul was. He faced his situation in honesty, came with hope and determination, and was met with understanding and acceptance. I am sure this was life-affirming for him.

As we continued to talk, Paul said he had told his brother, Steven, that he was gay several months before, and that Steven had encouraged him to tell me. I was gratified that they both trusted that I would understand. It was not difficult for me to do so. I had loved Paul for all the years of his life. Now he had taken me into his confidence, and trusted me

157

with a most intimate and important part of his inner life.

He was still my same, beloved son.

Now I was crying again, as I realized the kind of misunderstanding and discrimination he would surely experience as a gay person. Though to me he was still my fine, talented, caring son, to many Paul would be first and only a homosexual.

As we finished our conversation, Paul asked, "Do you think I should tell Dad? Or do you want to tell him?"

"I think he would appreciate it if you told him," I said.

And that was the way it was.

Angus and I are fortunate. Our faith is in the boundless love of God for all persons. We are confident that none are excluded. We find reason for this faith in the words and acts of Jesus himself. We believe that Paul's sexuality is not his choice but a given. An orientation. We believe his sexuality is not a mistake or perversion, but that, like all sexuality, it is a gift to be used in a loving and responsible way.

It was and is our intention to honor the trust that Paul has placed in us, and to support him in his continuing growth as the person God intended him to be.

✳ ✳ ✳

Not all reactions are like Catherine's, however. Too often, a gay man or lesbian's coming out is met with denial, accusations, and antagonism. We heard many of these stories during the campaign. One especially hits close to home.

A fine, wonderful young man tried to explain himself to his own mother and father (well, to his mother. He was afraid to tell his father). He told his mother he is a gay man and that he had been in a committed relationship but that his partner died of AIDS.

His mother's reaction was the opposite of that addressed in Catherine Cameron's story.

In fact, the son once thought they were working things out, but apparently that was not the case. He called her after watching the groundbreaking episode of the sitcom *Ellen*, when Ellen DeGeneres came out as a gay woman.

"Mom, did you hear?" he asked. "Did you see the show?"

"You promised me you would never talk about that disgusting subject again," she said. "It's a good thing you live far away from us."

I believe the mother loves her son, and he certainly deserves her love. But she is more afraid and concerned with what her church friends and the people in her community will think. At one time she begged him to leave his home in Florida and come back to the Northeast where he was born and raised so she could get him "degayed."

That's a terrible response. His heart is broken too. As much as I love him and as much as he deserves his mother's comfort, it is denied him. No one can take her place, and she doesn't seem able to see him as he is: a wonderful, loving son.

One of my favorite stories from the campaign was about a man named Bobby and what we call "The Case of the Potted Transplant."

Bobby was young and gay and had AIDS. He had turned to his family for comfort and love in his last days, and had been rebuffed. But Bobby was such a personable young man that he had many devoted friends who would never think of leaving him alone. They proved their devotion by caring for him in every way possible. In truth, they became his family, and Bobby entrusted them with his last wishes: that he be cremated and his ashes scattered over the ocean he loved.

When the time came, his wishes were carried out and Bobby's ashes floated free—but all was not well in Mudville. Bobby's family suffered an attack of conscience and demanded his ashes, insisting that he be buried in the family plot. Strange how they rejected him in life and demanded him in death.

Well, Bobby's friends were truly taken aback. Fearful that they might violate some arcane law or statute, they devised a plan where all could remain hidden. With great care, they constructed a small box the size of a cremains container. When the container was completed, they went to Kmart and bought a bag of potting soil. Into the make-believe cremains container went the dirt, onto the container went the cover, and the whole thing was delivered to the family.

Very shortly after, Bobby's legal survivors ceremoniously lowered the box of potting soil into the ground, leaving all concerned satisfied. Especially Bobby.

Eloise met so many wonderful people in her work within the church. They have tried to bring fresh air into the pews, and foster an opening of the minds and hearts of those who for all their lives have clung to certain myths and beliefs about homosexuality.

One such person was Bill, a longtime Methodist minister, now retired, who sympathized with our cause and did what he could to help.

Bill recalled an experience he'd had years before, while

he was in seminary school. He and two or three other students were walking across campus discussing their recent studies—how the Gospels came to be written and the meaning of certain passages therein.

Bill was more or less ruminating out loud when he said, "You know that passage in Luke, where Jesus said to Peter that Peter would betray him 'three times before the cock's crow'? I wonder if Jesus might have meant before the third watch in the night. The Romans named their watches of the night, and called the last watch, the one that ended in the morning, the 'cock's crow.'"

One of Bill's companions turned to him, his face red. He jabbed his index finger in Bill's face, and said with great agitation, "If you say anything else like that, you're going straight to hell. Don't you know Jesus meant exactly what he said? A rooster was going to crow. How dare you try to interpret Holy Scripture like that!"

Bill let the whole thing go, for he understood where it came from. As churches grapple with the matter of homosexuality, he explained to us, people offset their fear by taking every word of the Bible literally. But when pressed to explain discrepancies, contradictions, and some words of Scripture, they trip themselves up. We saw that ourselves over the course of the campaign: people who quoted long passages from the Bible about love and acceptance but who didn't think twice about cutting homosexuals off like lepers. And if we called them on it, they stammered and ran.

Eloise believes it must be a great fear that afflicts them. They would be bereft if they could not have the Bible to back up their arguments that a sexual orientation different from their own is a "sin." And it would seem that their own faith is not strong enough to stand up to any questioning.

It's the old domino theory again. If one portion of their carefully built tower of defense were to fall, then might not the entire structure?

Says Eloise: "I don't know if I'm going to live long enough to see any of that change. The only thing that's going to change them, I think, is embalming fluid."

＊ ＊ ＊

In February 1995 the AIDS Service Agency sent me to a middle school to take part in an AIDS education program for seventh-graders. This school was courageous and forward-thinking in its effort to shed light on an important concern. The two-part program would feature a young man with AIDS speaking of his illness, and a mother (me) speaking of the loss of a family member to the disease.

The AIDS patient was Steve Corum, a handsome young man with startling blue eyes. He stood out not because he had his own driver (he was unable to drive because of his illness) but because he was completely bald. This seemed strange to those who met him casually and didn't know his history, especially since his face looked so young.

Steve and I hit it off immediately, and we set to our tasks with eagerness. The students were so attentive and considerate of his condition and my loss. They were bright and asked perceptive questions, which made us feel that this day would be productive. The plan was for us to spend the entire school day there, speaking to each 50-minute class. The first three moved along smoothly. Steven was clearly engrossed in this effort, feeling he was contributing something to this world that he would have to leave soon.

Midway through the day, snow started to fall. Now, in

North Carolina, a snowflake is the same as an emergency alarm in the public school system. What if the buses can't get everyone home? What if we're stranded by an icy road or have to stay inside the school? Within five minutes of the first snowflake, administrators made a decision: All classes would be compressed into 14 minutes each so that the buses could depart early and avoid disaster.

This was fine with me, and knowing that Steven's message was much more important for the students to hear, I let him have the 14 minutes. And he tried. Oh, how he tried. His spirit was so strong, but his body had no reserves against stress. Steven made it through the first compressed class without any apparent problems, and, seemingly, the second 14-minute session went well.

The bell had rung, and the students had started to file out of the trailer classroom. The bustling and excitement of the snowfall was taking its toll on the day, and Steven was not exempt. From across the room I heard a great thud and a shout from his driver: "Steven!" Turning toward the sound, I saw Steven on the floor next to the teacher's desk, curled up in the fetal position, his thin frame convulsing as I had once seen Mark's do.

In that instant I was transported back to Mark's hospital room in West Palm Beach, Fla., and watched again as the life began to ebb from my son. As if reenacting the whole memory, I went to Steven's feet and held them. The volunteer driver held his upper body. As we tried to help him, those wonderful and caring students stood quietly and filed out of the room with nary a foolish gesture or word.

The EMTs came and took Steven to the hospital. The school closed, the buses ran, and, of course, the snow ceased. I started home, about 10 miles away. The prospect of being alone with this flashback still so vivid in my mind made me uneasy. Where to go? I didn't want to burden my family with this distress. I didn't know where Eloise was. So I drove to the AIDS Service Agency, which had sent me into this arena. The director, Cullen Gurganus, was there, and immediately saw my distress. I don't think I could even articulate what happened at first. But as I blurted out the essence of the day he just opened his big arms and I cried my heart out. Sometimes it's easier to burden a relative stranger than someone close to you.

Steven died sometime after that awful day, but not before he knew he had made a tremendous impact on the lives of those youngsters. They wrote him many letters telling him how much his talk had meant to them and how it had changed their thinking and made them aware of many dangers.

In that sense, Steven made his mark on the world. "I am the red ribbon," he used to say. "Wear it for me."

✳ ✳ ✳

All of us have experienced mystical occurrences at one time or another. We call them coincidences or "one of those funny, unexplained things." Sometimes we pay them no attention, but often we are fortunate and recognize and cherish them.

Many times after Eloise and I met we were aware of such happenings. First off, the way we met through similar tragedies and the fact that our lives had taken such different, although parallel, paths.

Both of our husbands were leaders in their fields, but Earl Vaughn was a liberal Democrat and Harry Clarke a conservative Republican. Eloise came from a conservative religious background, while I was raised a Christian Scientist—certainly outside of the mainstream.

We are close in age, so we have shared world memories like Franklin Roosevelt, World War II, and jitterbugging to big bands. We each raised four children during the era of stay-at-home moms. Both of us were teachers because back then it was OK to combine that with child-rearing.

Outside of these activities, Eloise avidly and devotedly supported Earl's political activities. I just as fervently followed my theatrical bent, performing as an actress and teaching theater arts. I was never politically astute or interested in such an arena. I was probably a drawback to my husband in that way. I remember a time when Harry ran for the local school board. We went to a rally about his candidacy and someone sashayed up to me and said, "We hope you're going to be working hard for his election."

"Probably not," I responded. "I think Harry is much too good a man for the political arena."

My reasoning was—and is—that politics is more about taking than giving, and I loved my husband too much to see him enter a lion's den. At any rate, he didn't win the race. He was much too honest and straightforward for the local pols.

All of these threads that Eloise and I found between us built a continuous, spiderlike web of connections. That both of our sons were named Mark was just a coincidence; Mark was one of the most popular names in the early 1960s. But that was just the beginning.

Sam Johnson, a Raleigh attorney, had known Earl Vaughn since young adulthood. Johnson also knew Harry Clarke and drove him to the airport the night he died in that fateful plane crash. In fact, Sam had urged Harry to stay in Raleigh that night

Yet our two husbands never knew each other, to our knowledge. Sometimes we like to think that maybe they did, and we imagine them together somewhere, at the North Carolina legislative building, or maybe at a bar nearby, sipping Scotch and saying at some point that they have to get home to their wives.

And we like to think that our two Marks are somewhere up there directing us, watching and laughing with pleasure at what we are doing and the special friendship their two moms have developed.

We have come to believe that there was something else at work in MAJIC—that our campaign was more than politics and fund-raisers. Someone had put us together, and out into the world.

During summer 1996, Eloise received a call from Virginia Gunn, an old friend of her son Mark. Mark had been gone six years, and we were in the middle of the MAJIC campaign. Eloise had sent some clippings about our activities to Virginia. A couple of days later Virginia called, her voice full of excitement, awe, and disbelief. Here's the story in Eloise's own words:

"Did Mark ever tell you about 'magic'?" Virginia asked, *her voice filled with a breathless expectation I could feel over the phone.*

"No," I said. "I don't believe I ever heard him speak of it."

"Well, when I received your letter and read the newspaper and magazine clippings you sent," she said, "my heart nearly stopped and the hair on my arms bristled. 'Magic' was our password. Nobody knew about it but us. How did you

happen to choose that word for the name of your campaign?"

I told her how we had chosen it, then Virginia proceeded to tell me their story. And it was my turn to have my heart nearly stop and the hair on my arms to bristle.

It was a blue-skied, low-humidity, bright morning in south Georgia, sometime in 1975. Mark Vaughn, then a news producer for Atlanta station WAGA, was accompanying Virginia, who was a reporter, on a shoot for that evening's 6 o'clock news.

The TV station van was loaded with the necessary photographic and technical equipment they needed. Mark was driving, and on the radio was a band called Pilot singing its hit "Magic."

As usual, Virginia and Mark sang along with the radio, hamming it up and laughing.

"That's it!" Mark said when it was over.

"That's what?" Virginia asked.

"Whichever of us dies first," Mark said, "will use the word 'magic' as a password to contact the other one from the other side."

"We are magic, you and I," Virginia said. "We'll always be magic."

And so they continued on with their assignment in good spirits. As Mark was setting up all the equipment, some problem developed with the wires, and for a moment, the good cheer they carried in with them had blown out of the room.

Virginia looked over and said, "Hey! It's magic!" Mark shook his head and smiled, and almost immediately the confidence they had on the ride down was restored.

Later, reviewing the tape they had shot, Virginia was complaining about her reporting skills. Mark sped up the tape and said, "It's magic, Virginia," and she began to laugh in spite of her self-doubt.

And so it went, for the next couple of years. "Magic" became a password between them. Whenever something wasn't going well or when anything went very well, they would look at each other and say "It's magic" and have to smile.

Virginia got married to a famous and very busy author. They moved to St. Simon's Island off the coast of Georgia, and Virginia continued her TV work for a while, shuttling back and forth to the studio in Atlanta.

Eventually, after Mark had suffered an unusually serious bout of hepatitis, he took a leave of absence and went to St. Simon's to take care of Virginia's menagerie of animals and to help keep the big, airy house going while Virginia and her husband traveled.

When Mark began to feel sicker, he came home to Raleigh. He didn't know it then, but he would never return to his by-then beloved island or share any more adventures with Virginia, his "magic" friend.

Instead, he would leave us too soon...and then, in an eerie yet comforting way, keep a promise to a friend, and remind us that he hadn't really left us at all.

✳ ✳ ✳

For my part, the outstanding "mystical" occurrence I experienced came as the first anniversary of MAJIC's first rally—the Mother's Day rally—approached.

Much had passed that was, for me, earth shaking. The election was over. So much work and effort seemed to have been for naught. Self-examination was not pleasant. Had I been a fool?

About this time, I was reading a book about second sight, written by Dr. Judith Orloff, a psychiatrist in Los Angeles and a self-acknowledged clairvoyant. The fact that she is a psychiatrist legitimized the topic of clairvoyance in my mind, and I have always been interested in the paranormal anyway.

Of everyone in my family, Mark was always the most receptive to my belief in the unknown and unexplained. Love is not logical, we agreed. Hate is not logical. Yet, we accept them as reality.

That night, as I was reading, my eye fell upon a bookcase that I have near my reading chair. It's a barrister-type case, with glass in front of the shelves. The lower shelf was empty except for some memorabilia. For the first time, for some reason I noticed a little piece of yellowed paper. I was curious, but because the bookcase is difficult to open and sometimes the glass casing falls loose, I didn't look any closer.

Several nights later I was reading again and reached a point in the book where the author writes about the death of her mother. She talks about her belief in the afterlife, the form it takes, and the possibility of messages from beyond. It was interesting but scary stuff.

It was time to go to bed. My eye fell again to that piece of yellow paper, still visible on that lower bookshelf. Something moved me. I put the book down, got down on the floor—which at this stage in my life is no easy feat—lifted the glass case, reached in, and pulled out that piece of construction paper.

Sure enough, in Mark's little first-grade hand was printed: "Mark C."

And in my hand was written a year: 1969. Now remember, this was 1997. I've made five major moves since 1969.

I turned the paper over, and on the front was a childish drawing of a tulip. I opened up the paper. It was a folded, handmade greeting card. In the middle of it, on lined paper children use to learn to write their names, were these words: "I love you. Happy Mother's Day."

I cried and I cried and I cried. Not from sadness, but from affirmation. It was what a friend of mine calls a message. And I was in the fortunate state of mind to recognize it was just that—an affirmation that love lasts and love can be unconditional.

Love isn't always unconditional, but it can be. Mark's for me and mine for him remain that way.

I wrote to Jesse Helms again. The first letter was written as a friend. This one, written after I had received his response and changed my life in so many ways because of it, came from a different Patsy Clarke. This Patsy had moved to another place in her mind, and in her heart.

Since receiving Jesse's letter, I had left much of what I had known far behind me to travel around the state and country, speak of my son, and meet people who sympathized, understood and, like me, yearned to see attitudes toward gays and lesbians changed.

It was a journey Jesse will never take. So I wanted to tell him what I had seen.

Dear Jesse,

I'm not sure if it is proper to call you Jesse anymore. When I last wrote it was as one who held you to be a friend. And, of course, you were a friend to my husband Harry. No question about it. And he to you. And now here I am, his widow, in a position of opposition. I guess that's what this letter is all about.

It has been almost exactly a year since we last exchanged letters. I wonder if you even remember my writing to you about my son Mark and his death from AIDS. For some reason, I feel compelled to tell you about what has happened to my thinking as a result of your answer to me.

I believe that if you had just said, "I'm so sorry," I would have retained my belief that Senator Helms was basically a kind human being. When I read your response saying that "the Bible judges homosexuality, I do not" and that you were sorry that Mark had chosen to play Russian roulette with his sexuality, I sat down in my chair and let the tears flow. The tears were for what I perceived as my ineptitude in reaching your heart. I kept saying to myself, over and over, "He didn't understand. He didn't understand."

The sense of helplessness that I felt at that time finally turned to a reexamination of beliefs and opinions I had long held—beliefs about political stands, about human beings who are different from myself, about many things I had simply taken for granted. Being part of mainstream, conservative American life for so many years had seemed comfortable and right, until my very being was forced to consider differently.

In a way, Senator, I wish you had simply written, "I'm sorry" in response to my letter. I could have remained sad, but secure, in my comfortable belief that you were beneficent in your view of other human beings; however, in another way I am grateful that you wrote to me as you did. It caused me to question the source and validity of the words you used in referencing the gay community with their "disgusting, revolting behavior."

I remembered my son. There was nothing disgusting or revolting about his behavior. He was honorable, kind, and accepting of differences in other human beings. The young man who was his partner has the highest of life principles. As I journeyed back through these memories, I began to question myself for accepting such opinions as you expressed in your letter. I searched out biblical writings and opinions on many of the concerns, but mostly I searched out my own heart. Believe me, this has not been easy, but it has been enlightening.

So, now, I find myself as a founding mother of Mothers Against Jesse in Congress (MAJIC), actively opposing your reelection. I can hardly believe this. I have always voted for Jesse Helms. I have always been a Republican. To change my life at age 67 is shocking to me, but so is the lesson you have taught me. It would have been infinitely easier to have grieved for Mark, put the loss behind me, and gotten on with my life as so many have suggested I do. But I can't. I offered you a quote from Patrick Henry in my last letter. This time I tender one from J.R. Lowell: "They are slaves who fear to speak for the fallen and the weak." I am trying to unslave my mind and heart from the rigid thought patterns I accepted for so long

Frankly, the freedom I have gained is heavy at

times. I would have preferred to cook Sunday dinners for my grandchildren, to travel a bit, do my needlework, and rest on the past. But the strongest principle that Harry and I taught at the kitchen table was that with every ounce of freedom comes a pound of responsibility.

This letter has wandered some. Forgive that, if you can.

Patsy Clarke

* * *

What I said in that letter remains true today, even as Eloise and I have moved on. Eloise has since bought a house in the mountains, where she can find rest and peace. I went back to the audition calls and was cast in some plays that gave me a chance to concentrate in an old and familiar way.

But neither of us has been able to put the experiences of the past few years behind us. It was rather like graduating from college. The educational experience of the MAJIC campaign and the time after has forever changed us. It continues to both motivate and influence us as we move further along in our lives.

It's true, what I said to Jesse Helms in my second letter. I really would have preferred to spend these years cooking Sunday dinners for my grandchildren, traveling, doing my needlework, and resting on the past...anything but becoming a political activist.

But that was not meant to be. And I cannot say that I am sorry.

ROLL CALL OF MAJIC MOTHERS

Patsy Munroe Clarke, 72, lost her son Mark to AIDS in 1994. A 52-year resident of North Carolina, she lived in Asheville and now lives in Raleigh. For more than 37 years, she was married to Harry Clarke, a prominent businessman and member of the Republican Party. Clarke served on the St. Joseph's Hospital Foundation for four years and taught theater and speech at the University of North Carolina, Asheville, for 10 years. She raised four children and has three grandchildren. She is a cofounder of MAJIC with Eloise Vaughn.

Kay Best Daughtry, 76, lost her son Michael to AIDS in 1994. Raised in Goldsboro, N.C., she has been married for 53 years. She worked for the Department of Public Instruction and Chamber of Commerce in both Raleigh and Goldsboro, and was an administrative assistant to Gov. Jim Hunt for eight years. She is past president of the North Carolina Democratic Women and was the first woman elected to the Garner Town Board, where she served three two-year terms.

Harriet Grand, 60, is the mother of a gay son. A native of Pennsylvania, she has lived in Raleigh for 33 years. She is an active volunteer with the Alliance of AIDS Services. She raised three children and has four grandchildren.

Gerry Guess, 59, is the mother of a gay daughter, Carol, a published novelist. A native of Illinois, Gerry lives in Chapel Hill. She read about MAJIC in *The Daily Tar Heel* newspaper and became the group's first financial contributor.

JoAnne Harvey, 48, lost her brother, William Thomas Harvey, to AIDS in 1994. She was born in Burlington, N.C., and has lived in Raleigh for 19 years. She is the director of the Vacation Bible School at the Edenton Street United Methodist Church, and served as the chair of its Children's Council program. She has worked as a vocation rehabilitation evaluator for the Alamance and Wake County Departments of Mental Health.

Gertrude "Trudy" Hogarth, 78, lost her son Bill to AIDS in 1995. Born in Henderson, N.C., she has lived in Cary for 50 years. She worked in the North Carolina Department of Agriculture, under Gov. Kerr Scott, for nine years. She has served as president of the local women's club and of the women's club at St. Paul's Episcopal Church, where she has been a member since 1958. Her husband, James Hogarth, was elected mayor of Cary in 1963 and served on the town council for 12 years.

Pat Johnson, 67, was born in North Carolina and has lived in the Raleigh area for well over 20 years. After receiving a nursing degree from the University of North Carolina, Chapel Hill, she went on to teach nursing at UNC and on the community college level for 19 years. She sponsored an inmate at the

North Carolina Correctional Institute for Women, and is a volunteer at the AIDS Service Agency in Raleigh.

Vernelle Ports Long, 75, is the mother of a gay daughter. She has lived in North Carolina for 13 years. She has been married for 50 years to a Methodist minister; her father, brother, and brother-in-law are Methodist ministers as well. She worked for 18 years as a public elementary school teacher, and is a published author who last finished *Lay Liturgist Library of Calls to Worship, Congregational Prayers and Benedictions.* She has been a leader in Parents, Families, and Friends of Lesbians and Gays.

Stephanie Marshall, 80, lost her son Kevin to AIDS when he was 45.

Eloise Maddry Vaughn, 68, lost her son Mark to AIDS in 1990. A lifelong resident of North Carolina, she now lives in Raleigh. A graduate of the University of North Carolina, Chapel Hill, she taught junior high school for 15 years, and was a receptionist at the North Carolina State Legislature for six years. She is the widow of Earl Vaughn, a former state supreme court judge. Vaughn has been a member of the Democratic Women for 45 years, a member of the Junior Woman's Club for 18 years, and a member of the Edenton Street United Methodist Church for 29 years. She raised four children, and has six grandchildren. She is a cofounder of MAJIC with Patsy Clarke.

Anne Thompson Walker, 70, lost her son Glenn to AIDS in 1993. She was born in Durham and moved to Rocky Mount, where she lived for 25 years. After 10 years in

Virginia, she returned to Durham in 1991. She is the wife of Marshall Walker, a semiretired Baptist minister. She worked as an administrative assistant to him when he served as the director of Associational Missions. She is also a church organist at Three Rivers Baptist Church in Durham, N.C. She is the mother of three sons and six grandchildren.